MOTHER EVE'S GARDEN CLUB

Rita,

As you and I
both love sisters
I thought you might
enjoy this little book -

Fondly

Mary Frances

LAJOYCE MARTIN

MOTHER EVE'S GARDEN CLUB

MULTNOMAH
Sisters, Oregon 97759

MOTHER EVE'S GARDEN CLUB

Published by Multnomah Books
a part of the Questar publishing family

© 1993 by LaJoyce Martin

International Standard Book Number: 0-945564-73-2

Cover illustrations by Mike Lester

Cover design by Bruce DeRoos
Edited by Shari MacDonald
and, Liz Heaney

Printed in the United States of America

For information:
QUESTAR PUBLISHERS, INC.
POST OFFICE BOX 1720
SISTERS, OREGON 97759

93 94 95 96 97 98 99 00 01 — 10 9 8 7 6 5 4 3 2 1

DEDICATION

This book is dedicated to the seven sisters who have kept
a round-robin letter going between themselves
for almost half a century:
letters of advice, sisterly chat, and encouragement.
Each time the seven-letter packet makes its full circuit,
a sister takes out her old letter
and puts a new one in its place.

My Mother is one of those sisters who has kept love's
golden chain unbroken.

For Guytie Mae, Lorene, Adele, Laverne,
Louella, Gwendolyn, and Frankie

CONTENTS

Welcome to the Garden Club

I've always wanted a sister.

Sisters are special. Sometimes they can be the most wonderful, loveable, thoughtful friends in the world. They share their dollar-a-bottle perfume. They bind up the pain under your ribs with an understanding smile. When they see you crying, they unspool a few yards of bathroom tissue for you to blow your nose on.

At other times, sisters can make you miserable. They show you up. They tell you what to do. They make bad choices in life, and all you can do is watch them suffer.

As I thought about it, I realized that I really *do* have sisters. I have ties to every woman who has ever lived, right back to the rib-built original. We are all part of Mother Eve's Garden Club. We're clinging to her fig leaf skirt, wearing her hand-me-down genes. The mud we are made of binds us together, like stick-together spaghetti in the kettle of humanity.

Biblical sisters are a lot like biological ones. Sometimes they're loveable, sometimes hateable. And sometimes they learn lessons the hard way. (Sound like anyone you know?) Not all of our dusty sisters would win a beauty contest in a pretty-is-as-pretty-does run-off. Halos are hard to find in this bunch. Then again, halos aren't required in Mother Eve's Garden Club.

Looking into the Bible, I found the sisters I had always wanted. I even saw a bit of myself in them. Maybe you will, too. Time alters lifestyles and cultures, but human nature never changes. The sisters who march across history's pages met with the same Goliaths we face today. And they responded in much the same way.

So come join the Garden Club. It's filled with women who will encourage, challenge, and teach you.

Just the sort of thing you'd expect from a sister.

MOTHER EVE'S GARDEN CLUB

David said to Abigail, "Praise be to the LORD,
the God of Israel, who has sent you
today to meet me.
May you be blessed for your good judgment
and for keeping me from bloodshed this day
and from avenging myself with my own hands."
1 Samuel 25:32-33

Abigail

OUR SISTER ABIGAIL really knew how to handle men.

She had charm. It came naturally to her. There weren't any finishing schools out in the desert, or modeling classes. Nobody taught her how to smile for the judges and wave elbow-elbow, wrist-wrist. Her beauty was more than skin deep. It came from inside. It was *bone* deep.

One man in particular cast his eye on Abigail. He was one of the richest land owners in the state, and was used to getting what he wanted. As usual, he did. And they lived...*unhappily* ever after.

It turned out that Bridegroom Nabal was one of the devil's boys. He threw temper tantrums and fell into drunken stupors on a regular basis. Abigail memorized the symptoms: oppressive silences, raving tirades, messy hangovers. When he drank himself sick, she was there to clean it up. Through it all, her sweet spirit never soured.

One day a young ranch hand panted up to tell Abigail a frightful story. Servants of a man named David had come to Carmel to ask her tightfisted, loose-tongued husband for something to munch on.

It seemed their boss, Mr. David, had spread his security blanket over Nabal's herdsmen when they were out in the wilderness. Now, he naturally assumed that Nabal would return the consideration. But in one long, run-on sentence, Nabal thundered that all Jerusalem would pay before he'd give *his* bread, *his* meat, and *his* water to a bunch of roving outlaws. Bad move.

David left with empty hands and a full craw. Some of *his* words were a bit off-color themselves.

Abigail's mind turned somersaults and cartwheels. She knew David would come to settle the score, wiping all of Nabal Industries off the map and filling the cemetery with monogrammed headstones. She did a quick memory check on her supplies. Cellar? Full. Smokehouse? Full. (She'd baked ahead for her husband's men.) You've got to hand it to her. This sister was an organizer. Servants scurried to her command.

"Fetch those two hundred loaves out of the warming oven. Now grab the two hundred fig cakes. A load of raisins. Five fat sheep. Two skins of wine. Pack it all—quickly!"

With the speed of a fast-food chef, she saw that the whole moving van of grub was packed and ready for special delivery. It was a prudent move.

By this time, David had already started Carmel-ward. He was spitting fireworks. But Abigail was ready, and she went out to meet him. When she came upon David and his men, Abigail quickly got off her donkey and bowed down before him.

"Blame me for everything," she begged, trying to set up a roadblock with her words. "I didn't see the young men you sent. I'm sorry. I would have felt honored to fill your food order."

Her eyes dropped in humble apology. When she looked up again, David's fury had sprung a small leak.

But idle chatter would not be enough to sway him, and sage Abigail knew it. She searched her mental files. What was something that would arouse David's interest, stimulate his mind? A slingshot. That's it!

At the mere mention of the word, Abigail knew she would have David's full attention. Once again, he would be a carefree lad with his childhood weapon in hand, whistling his way to faraway hills filled with bears, lions…the nine-foot giant he had killed with his customized stone launcher.

So Abigail said, "Sir, God will sling the souls of your enemies as out of the middle of a sling!" Painting on the canvas of his mind, she reminded him of one of his greatest victories, of better days, bolstering his spirits when he needed it the most.

"Watch your enemies go sailing away, David!" her words implied. "They're hitting the ground with a thud. Running, falling before you. You're the winner!" She made him remember the pleasant so he would forget the unpleasant. Smart woman.

As a smile pulled at the corners of David's mouth, Abigail knew he could see and taste the sweet triumph of victory. He felt good again. Not angry or vindictive or bitter. Just good. He wouldn't want to botch that feeling with regrets. Abigail's household would live.

David blessed Abigail for her wisdom. Then he took the goodies and dismissed her with a well-earned, "Go in peace."

Exonerated, relieved, and free from fear, Abigail turned back toward the haunts of home. Meanwhile, back at the ranch, the man she had fought so valiantly to save lay sleeping in a drunken coma.

But God took matters into his own hands. Ten days later, Abigail found her besotted man dead. She was no longer the devil's daughter-in-law. God himself gave the autopsy report in the Bible: Nabal's heart became as a stone, its valves and arteries unable to contract or expand.

Someone handed the obituary to David. As he read it, he recalled with great tenderness the beautiful woman who had talked to him about the slingshot. She'd kept him from stupidly killing a lot of innocent people. Under his breath, David thanked God. And Abigail.

The bud of an idea began to bloom. Why not invite this wise and gracious woman to be his wife? David sent her a Valentine greeting and proposed. He wanted an immediate ceremony. It was like a fairy-tale: from the devil's family to God's.

Haste was no stranger to Abigail, but this time she *really* hurried. She bowed with her face to the ground, asking for the privilege of washing the feet of David's servants. It was a heart-stealing sight.

She'd proven herself loyal and kept a right attitude through all of life's hard knocks. Now God had something else in mind for her, and so did David. Promotion day had come.

When David was crowned king of Israel, Abigail shared in the coronation. She was a natural queen. After all, she'd demonstrated royal wisdom all along. She understood men—their strengths and their weaknesses. When things got tough, she appealed to David's noble nature. She poured liniment onto his troubled spirit and brought him back to the man he wanted to be.

Abigail had more than charm. She had prudence. Whether she lived with a devil or a saint, she wore her queenly qualities like a jeweled crown.

And that's the kind of beauty that goes bone deep.

That's the kind of beauty that goes *soul* deep.

Lord, let some of Abigail's prudence inoculate me! Endow me with wisdom to know when to speak and when to keep quiet. Show me how to help those I love in their areas of weakness. And let my spirit reflect the beauty of your love for me.

Coming up to them at that very moment,
she gave thanks to God and spoke about the child
to all who were looking forward
to the redemption of Jerusalem.

Luke 2:38

ANNA

GETTING OLDER DOESN'T seem so bad when you look at our sister, Anna.

She was our December sister. With snow white hair, soft wrinkled hands and a withered body, Anna was great of age, but young in hope.

One thing is certain: she wasn't the sort of pensioner to sit around and watch the mailbox for her Social Security check. She was busy and active. She made herself useful.

Anna knew better than anyone that moments are not for keeps; they are for spending. They have an expiration date. Just like the leftover meat in the Israelite's quail pail, moments spoil if they're hoarded. You've got to use them...or lose them.

"Care for the little moments, and the big moments will take care of themselves." That was Anna's philosophy, and she'd waited a lifetime for the one big moment that she knew would come.

She'd lived many years, and time on the old wind-up clock was beginning to run out. The pendulum would soon stand still. Leaves from life's calendar lay in the top drawer of Anna's memory. They included some dark days, but Anna refused to let life's tragedies take away her glimpses of heaven. She wasn't given to pulling yesterday's clouds over today's sunshine.

The hardest blow had come years before, when she gave up her young husband to death after only seven years of marriage. That page of her life was way down in the stack now, dried and faded.

At the time of her husband's death, Anna could have stayed where she was. She might have raised an herb garden or woven fabric at the loom. She could have remarried or gone into business for herself. She might have sold purple cloth, managed an inn, or even provided home health care.

But she chose none of those things. Instead, she decided to move next door to God. She liked having him for a close neighbor. For the rest of her life, she spent every single day at God's house. She wanted to live a plane apart from worldly preoccupations, so she fasted and prayed, night and day. She saw it as a glorious privilege, not a forced monotony.

She waited for her one big moment, pitying those who never shared in the service of Jehovah or felt the hallow of his daily presence. Anna didn't count the days; she made her days count.

She became a prophetess and pored over scrolls of the Law and Prophets. She studied the Old Testament Scriptures by the hour. She memorized the Holy Writ until it was tattooed on her heart and branded into her mind.

"For unto us a child is born, unto us a son is given..."

She watched each mother who came and went with her newborn, searched every face. Could this be the one? Any day now, the Messiah would come just as Isaiah had said.

She had a feeling in her brittle old bones. Ignoring the high mileage on her odometer, Anna kept right on going. She knew she hadn't reached her destination yet. She wouldn't give up. She'd limp on in, if necessary.

Her sixth sense missed nothing. Lately, she'd seen old Simeon coming to the temple with a new spring in his step and an aura of expectancy. He'd even made a strange proclamation: he claimed he wouldn't die until he had seen the Lord's Christ, and he said it with certainty.

Hmm.

But Simeon was sledding downhill toward the graveyard, too, racking up overtime on his life span. Whatever was going to happen, had to happen soon.

One day Anna walked into the temple to find old Simeon cradling a newborn child in his leathery arms. There was a rapturous light in his faded eyes. "Now I can die in peace!" he said. Then he conferred a praise-blessing on the infant, calling him "a light for revelation to the Gentiles," and "glory to your people Israel."

Anna drew closer to the child. Could it be he? The one she had waited a lifetime for? (If you close your eyes, you can see her holding out hungry arms for the glorious child.)

Jesus. The Messiah. He had come! It was the realization of her dream. All she had waited for had come to pass.

But Anna didn't stop there. She made the most of her moment. She wanted everyone to know about Jesus, and she made it her own personal responsibility to tell them about him.

"The Messiah is here! The One Isaiah told about. Wonderful. Counsellor. The Mighty God. The Everlasting Father. The Prince of Peace."

She put her voice in gear and "spoke about the child to all who were looking forward to the redemption of Jerusalem."

"He is alive! I saw him for myself. I *touched* him."

It was enough. She knew she could not hold the big moment forever. Her work was complete.

Anna would not live another three decades to see the healings or the miracles. She wouldn't hear his teachings and his promises. She probably wouldn't even be in the temple twelve years later when he confounded the doctors and lawyers with his words.

But she had touched him. That was sufficient.

The old and battered tent—like the tabernacle in the wilderness—had come to the end of its faithful service. It was time to pack away the portable dwelling and move on to a "house not made with hands eternal in the heavens." Anna could go in peace. Without clinging to lost yesterdays. With no sad goodbyes.

She had spent her moments well.

Lord, I want to make the most of each precious day. As I grow older, help me to be faithful like Anna. Help me live each moment to its fullest, then let it melt into the evening sunset as I await a brand-new morning.

Village life in Israel ceased,
ceased until I, Deborah, arose,
arose a mother in Israel.

Judges 5:7

Deborah

SOME PEOPLE SAY, "It's a man's world." But those words never came from Deborah's lips.

She knew from experience that circumstances can pitchfork women into the heat of life's worst battles. Literally. These female warriors often fight without high calibre ammunition, sophisticated communication systems, or even adequate training.

If we paint them with pastels in our mental coloring books, we're using the wrong Crayolas. These sisters deserve bold shades. We should picture them in red, white and blue, wearing purple hearts and green berets.

When we first see this sister, Moses and Aaron are already history. The Joshuas and Calebs had long since turned to dust. For twenty years, the sons of Israel had suffered cruel oppression at the hands of Jabin, king of Canaan. Now, something had to give.

The nation quaked with fear. They played Scramble. The enemy had nine hundred chariots of iron—Israel had zero. But Deborah saw the Creator as big enough to overcome the numerical odds. At a time when they needed strong leadership the most, no man was brave enough to step into Israel's headlines.

So God elected Deborah as judge.

Day after day, she held court under a palm tree. And day after day, she heard the same bitter complaints:

"Our crops have been vandalized."

"My daughter was kidnapped by King Jabin and taken for a slave in his palace."

"They drafted my husband as a woodcutter."

Judge Deborah gave counsel and encouraged her people, spreading her contagious courage and kindling enthusiasm for action. She was busier than a mother with quintuplets. But she knew that twenty years of torture couldn't be God's will. God is a God of victory, not defeat. A voice inside urged Deborah on: "Wake up, wake up, Deborah! It's time to take captive your captives."

So Deborah mustered an impromptu army of ten thousand men. She called a man named Barak to lead them, telling him the Lord would deliver the captain of the enemy's regiment into his hands.

"What?" questioned Barak. "With no war horses? No chariots? No weapons? With only ten thousand men bare-handed and on foot against Captain Sisera's nine hundred metal chariots and a multitude of trained soldiers?"

Judge Deborah and Captain Barak looked eyeball to eyeball. Both considered the ramifications of the battle, but each saw a different view.

Barak envisioned formidable iron tanks and more than enough weapons to wipe his small army off the map. In his mind's eye, he saw his empty-handed men without a round of munitions among the lot.

Deborah saw each man equipped with spiritual weapons of faith, prayer, and power. She pictured the enemy defeated by an innumerable host of angels.

When pressed, Barak balked. He'd only go on one condition: that the woman judge come along. He'd be the back-seat driver.

So Deborah agreed to go. She and Barak would stay together and pray together. But she warned that it wouldn't look good for him when a woman got the upper hand of the leader of the enemy battalion.

Even after Barak had given his word, Deborah had to stay after him to get him to move. He sat idling in neutral. "Get up," she ordered one morning. "Today is the day."

And so the war started. A storm broke over the enemy

troops. Captain Sisera parachuted from his chariot and ran for safety, leaving his troops to Barak's attack. Every man fell by the sword. Not a soul was left.

Meanwhile, the "safety" Sisera found was in a woman's tent. A clever sister named Jael sweet-talked him, saying, "Come, my lord, come right in. Don't be afraid." She gave him milk, covered him up...then finished him off, driving a nail through his temple as he slept.

Just as Deborah had predicted, a woman got the credit for ending the war.

It shouldn't be a surprise that God chose to add a woman to his register of judges, or that he delivered the enemy into a woman's hands. In any given situation, God will use the best person he can find. Even when circumstances seem to require a man, God may enlist a woman who is willing to follow his call.

History is laced with Deborahs: invincible soldiers who wage war against nine hundred obstacles and a multitude of demons. Some serve as lone women missionaries. Others go to church alone, fighting a spiritual battle single-handedly.

These women struggle on, squeezing money from the food budget for gasoline and patronizing garage sales for their children's school clothes. They collect double coupons and wear extra wraps to save on the fuel bill. Yet, all the while they cherish an inner knowledge: God is big enough to whip hatred, jealousy, bitterness...every enemy of the spirit.

Won't these sisters have a victory song to sing in heaven!

These women look past the seen to the unseen. They picture the garment finished before the material is cut from the bolt, taste the cookies before they are baked. They are the essence of Deborah.

I am reminded of a story about two painters who went to a hill outside a city. One painted the roof of a dilapidated shed in the valley below. The other looked out over the landscape and painted the sunset, his scene rich with the colors of an evening sky.

Deborah's vision was greater than that of either painter. Her eyes never focused on earth's dirty shingles or the toll of life's storms. Deborah saw *beyond* the sunset.

She saw the power of God.

Thank you, God, for Deborah, a woman like myself. Although she faced a great battle, you gave her the courage to fight incredible odds and win. I know you'll do the same for me. Life is a battle for me just now, and I need you by my side. Please grant me spiritual insight, Lord. For I know with your wisdom, I will come out victorious.

Then she said to him,
"How can you say, 'I love you,' when
you won't confide in me…?"

Judges 16:15

Delilah

THERE'S NO WAY around it. This woman was trouble.

We know there are at least seven things that are really detestable to God. He lists them in Proverbs 6. Four of those hates rounded up Delilah: her double-dealing tongue looped the rope around her neck, and her lying, evil-devising, and mischief-seeking lassoed her.

Now a two-faced friend is bad news, but a two-faced enemy brings *rigor mortis*. This lady was an enemy of the worst kind. She spit blackmail out of both sides of her mouth.

Samson was Delilah's "foe-beau." He was wanted by the Philistine Police Department for arson, vandalism and murder. He was an idol-god opponent. A Nazarite.

Delilah had heard some wild stories about her boyfriend. It seemed this superman could switch on his incredible strength at will. He upended a city gate and toted it away bareback, caught and turned three hundred foxes into running torches, and shredded a lion barehanded. He even slew a thousand men with a single piece of bone.

It didn't take Delilah long to find Samson's great weakness, but she couldn't quite pinpoint the source of his strength. With burrs under their saddles, the rulers of the Philistines each offered her eleven hundred pieces of silver to find Samson's "power main," short-circuit the current, and get it shut off.

That much silver would put her name alongside society's wealthy in the weekly newspaper, so Delilah accepted the job. She sat up nights formatting her plans.

Delilah invited Samson to an evening around the fireplace where she used every tactic she knew on the spiritual giant. A lot of money was up for grabs, here. No trick was too low. She used feminine charm, gimmicks, even deceit (falsehood fits a turncoat).

In the den, they played a game called "Where Is the Power Switch?" Like a child playing "I Spy," Delilah's search took her from cold to hot as she got closer to the fuse box. The game progressed over time as Samson gave her one answer after another.

"I mustn't be tied with thongs."

"My strength will be lost if I am bound with new ropes."

"If you weave my hair into a web, I will grow weak as any man."

Each time, Delilah called his bluff. And each time she appealed to him for his trust. Finally it came: the confession of a haircutless life.

Ah, yes. Uncut hair. It was a religious vow. And if Samson's hair was cut, he would be as weak as watered-down milk.

Well, this miss of mischief could take care of that. She invited Samson back one more time for some R and R. A little bedtime story, a soft lap, a sharp pair of scissors...and Samson would be plunged into darkness. He would be as useless as a lamp without a wick. Guided by gleeful hands, Delilah's shears went to work.

Like a douse of cold water, Delilah's cry of *"Philistines!"* pulled Samson from his sleep. He struggled to his feet, groping for the switch he had flipped on and off so many times before. The Power Switch.

Delilah had seen him do it before. Now she watched with mocking amusement. This time there would be no power. Seven locks of hair lay scattered about the room like so many broken filaments.

"I'll shake myself." The words came from his dry, sleep-lined mouth. "And then I'll be as good as new."

Delilah knew the truth.

Samson didn't.

His power line had been short-circuited by an under-handed woman and a pair of Philistine scissors. The men she had called put out Samson's eyes with a hot poker and jeered while they did it. He was blinded, both physically and spiritually. Delilah robbed him of all his valuables and left him bankrupt.

He was forced to grind away at the prison mill like an animal. Around and around he went. Day in...day out. Day in...day out. The Philistines turned the fire on high and left him to simmer.

Blind he might be, but he lifted his burned out sockets toward the sky and prayed. He was willing to give his life for one more surge of power. He wanted one last chance to flip the switch, and find out that it worked.

The Philistines called a victory rally. Delilah wouldn't have missed it for the world. She wanted to join in the ridicule of the strong man she had starred in dwarfing.

They brought Samson in. He couldn't see Delilah, daz-zling though she was in the new clothes she'd bought with money earned by evil. But he recognized that voice, that laugh. He would have known that sound anywhere.

She must have been the belle of the ball. Perhaps Samson heard the emcee introduce her to the jubilant crowd: "And this, ladies and gentlemen, is Lady Delilah, who for eleven hundred pieces of silver from each of our lords delivered the Israelite giant into our hands."

A roar of applause. Wolf whistles. Drum rolls.

Didn't anyone see Samson's lips moving? Didn't they check the pressure cooker?

"O Lord God, remember me. And strengthen me. Only this once."

The last charge of electricity in Samson's life outdid any of his previous jolts. He wrapped himself around the two middle pillars of Dagon's Temple as the current surged, toppling the hall of fame on three thousand people, including the traitoress.

And himself.

Delilah didn't live long enough to learn her lesson. But we can learn from her mistake. We can know that, while truth is worth more than it costs, a lie always costs more than it is worth.

Lord, don't let me be responsible for pulling another down. As mother, wife, daughter, sister, and friend...let me never give in to dishonest practices. Keep me true and aboveboard in all I do and say, and help me to honor you.

"...I will go to the king,
even though it is against the law.
And if I perish, I perish."

Esther 4:16

Esther

SOMETIMES REAL LIFE is more beautiful than a fairy-tale.

Esther's biography is made of bedtime story tapestry. It's non-fiction to the core, but reads like fiction and could as easily have begun, "Once upon a time." It has all the important elements of a prize-winning script: suspense, romance and conflict; crisis, climax and resolution.

In the city of Jerusalem lived a little girl named Hadassah, who was also called Esther. An orphan, she had been taken in by her cousin Mordecai, a man who loved her and raised her as if she were his very own daughter.

One day in March, a coup took place in the city. A foreign government took over and Haddasah, her cousin, and 9,998 others were taken captive and made slaves.

Her cousin Mordecai became a guard at the palace gate, the family found a nice place to live, and young Esther grew up in the city of Susa.

Then one day, a shocking story was broadcast over the news.

"We interrupt your day with this special news bulletin. Sources from the king's dispatch have confirmed that King Xerxes was wronged by his wife, Queen Vashti, earlier today when she disobeyed one of the king's direct commands. One royal insider quoted the king as saying, 'I am *really* ticked off.' More news after these messages."

All 127 states under the monarchy heard the bulletin. The scandal shocked everyone, and they all had an opinion about what should be done. Some said the queen should never be allowed into the palace again. Others said she should be quarantined. A few called for a restraining order. Finally, one of the king's wise men recommended that she be replaced with someone worthy of the position.

So the queen was ousted, and things calmed down a bit. For two years, Esther heard no more about it.

But then one day a messenger came thundering through the neighborhood with an important announcement:

"Hear ye! Hear ye! All single girls, young and fair-faced. There's to be a beauty contest!"

The winner would take all: the king, the tiara, the honeymoon suite in the mansion. She'd be crowned Miss Universe.

The old maids were beside themselves. They put spoons on their puffy eyelids, did aerobics to get in shape, even dressed ten years younger. Some joined Weight Watchers.

Every woman day-dreamed about what it would be like to win the royal lottery, to hit the jackpot, to call out, "Bingo!" As the winner, she'd have plenty of money and exclusive clothes. There would be countless servants and a chauffeured chariot with vanity plates.

Esther gave the matter little thought. After all, she wasn't a local girl. She was a P.O.W. Ethnic.

But a lovely face and gentle spirit has no place to hide. Someone noticed Esther and put her name on the contest ballot. Her cousin Mordecai insisted that she keep her nationality a secret, and she did.

As judging time drew near, Esther held all the winning tickets. The manager of the harem took a shine to her and put her in the best room in the house. He even appointed seven girl Fridays to see that she was well cared for.

The contest rules allowed each girl to choose anything she wanted to wear, in any color. She could fix her hair any way she wished, order any brand of perfume to match her personality. But Esther asked for nothing. Zilch. She didn't need anything. Not the gooey makeup. Not the special frills. Not even the gaudy jewelry.

Each contestant had her chance to march before the king, to try all her tricks and charms to impress him. Esther offered only herself. She used no additives. There was no hypocrisy, no stratagem. She had nothing to prove and nothing to lose.

When Esther walked in, the contest was over. She won by a landslide. Everyone's favorite, she finished the competition way out in front. After it was over, she married the king and put on the royal crown. And as a sign of his pleasure, he held a banquet and proclaimed a holiday in honor of Esther, his "star."

It's a great ending. But, wait…it isn't the end.

One day, Mordecai overheard two palace guards plotting to kill Esther's new husband, the king. He sent word to her, and she, in turn, was able to warn her husband. After a complete investigation, the conspirators were found guilty and hanged, and the king wrote down the incident in his diary.

Esther was quite happy. She didn't smell the garbage that fermented around tomorrow's corner.

The garbage started with a top dog in the kingdom, the man second in command to the king himself. Haman was a haughty smart-aleck who was jealous of Esther's cousin. He couldn't stand the sight of Mordecai, so he deliberately set out to get him in trouble.

Apparently, the officer with the malignant self-image wanted Esther's cousin to bow to him on command. Now, Mordecai wasn't trying to be rebellious or hard to get along with. He simply had a little rule: he wouldn't bow to anyone but God.

Sir Haman, the king's left-hand man, decided to get revenge. So he fixed up papers to kill all the foreigners who had been imported in the take-over—just so he could get the one Jewish man he hated. He wanted the one who wouldn't kowtow to him or kiss his feet.

Haman worked on his scheme for almost a year. He wrote and rewrote his proposal until he got the plan just right. He practiced his speech so many times, he had it memorized:

"Your Majesty, I know something you don't. While you are palace-sitting all day, I am out moving among the people, and I have found that we have some lawbreaking aliens sprinkled throughout all 127 of our states."

The king raised his eyebrows. He frowned at the word. "Lawbreakers?"

"Yes, Your Majesty. *Lawbreakers*. And if I were you, I wouldn't tolerate it. In fact, if you'll just turn everything over to me, I'll see that these enemies of yours are wiped off the map. Of course, I'll need a little money to get the job done. Nineteen-and-a-half million ought to be enough."

The ploy worked. Letters with the king's seal went out Federal Express.

The proclamation called for all Jews, young and old (including women and children) to be annihilated on March 14. Their possessions would be pay dirt for those who handled the details.

Sir Haman, pleased as punch with himself, went out for coffee with the king while everyone else in the empire scratched their heads and wondered, "What is going on?"

All of a sudden, Esther's family and friends were crying, and she didn't know why. Her cousin was sobbing aloud. He had taken off his good clothes, put on shabby ones, and appeared in public in his ragged attire.

Esther figured he needed something, so she sent him a nice suit. But Mordecai wouldn't wear it. Instead, he came to the gate weeping bitterly. Esther had someone ask him, "Why the deep depression?"

Mordecai sent an urgent cablegram to his cousin, along with a photostatic copy of Haman's plot, asking her to please go to her husband and to try to cancel the slaughter schedule.

Esther instantly whipped back a message, explaining that she was between a rock and a hard place. She hadn't seen the king for a month, and she couldn't just barge in, unannounced, to talk to him. Anyone who entered the inner court without an invite got the death sentence. That was one of the king's cardinal rules. No one had to be reminded what had happened to the last queen who had offended the king. How could she know whether he would be in a forgiving mood?

A Priority Mail packet brought one last answer. Mordecai warned Esther that she needn't think she would escape death just because she lived in the plushy palace. The decree applied to her entire nationality—including her highness. There was no tolerance. There were no exceptions. She had better speak up, Mordecai warned, or the Jews would be saved through another source and she would be history.

The letter ended, "P.S. Who knows, Esther? Maybe God put you in the palace just to save our lives."

It was a big decision for such small shoulders, but Esther knew what she had to do. It required all the courage she could muster, and she fasted and prayed for three days. On Day Three, Esther put on her best dress, the king's favorite, and went into the awesome inner court. As if urged on by an invisible force, she walked toward the king on his throne.

She trembled. Waited. Hoped.

The king held out his scepter.

"What do you want, my beautiful star? Whatever it is, you can have it. I'll divide the kingdom right down the middle if that's what you want."

Esther swayed and gave a tiny relieved smile. But she couldn't blurt out the whole gory story there at the throne. She needed time. So she told him she was cooking him something special and asked him to join her for dinner that night. "And," she tacked on, "Would you be so kind as to invite Officer Haman along, too?"

"No problem," said the king.

Esther felt better. But the job of saving her people was still in the future. She hadn't yet reached the city limits of her mission.

At the evening meal, the king looked at his beloved. She was still the apple of his eye.

"Isn't there something you wish," he asked, "little wife, star of my life? Just ask and you'll have it. I promise."

Just then, the cat got her tongue. (Maybe Haman, the toughy, was looking at her, making her lose her nerve.) So she postponed the request for one more day, one more dinner.

Sir Haman left the palace with a bragging spirit. He boasted to everybody he met about his riches, his kids, his job, his intelligence. But mostly he bragged that he—and he alone—had another invitation to dinner with the queen. And that meant he was important, with a capital *I*.

Nothing blotched Haman's ledger of happiness except the unbowing man at the gate, but all the credits to his name couldn't erase that one debit. Haman's wife and friends threw out a potpourri of suggestions. He liked one idea in particular and resolved to build a seventy-five-foot gallows to hang the impudent man on. He would then go on to Esther's dinner party and have himself a grand old time.

So Haman scared up a hammer and some nails from his workshop. While he worked, he planned his trip to the palace and rehearsed his speech to the king, asking for permission to hang the gate man.

That night, the king had insomnia. He couldn't sleep a wink and didn't know why. Nothing worked. He tried warm milk, soft music...even counting sheep. After awhile, he tired of staring, wide-eyed, at the ceiling. So he got up, put on his robe and slippers, and paced.

Maybe reading will help. That sometimes makes a body sleepy. He called for his diary.

As he leafed through his journal, the king found a record of something he had long since forgotten. It was about the man at the gate who had saved his life by warning him about a death plot. "Was that man ever rewarded?" he turned to the soldier standing ramrod straight nearby.

"No, my king."

Suddenly, a noise was heard coming from the hall. Sir Haman had come to talk with him. The king bid his highest officer to enter. Just as the man opened his mouth to ask his thought-worn question, the king turned the tables and asked him a question instead.

"What," the king wanted to know, "Should be done for a man the king wishes to honor specially?" He was looking for a payback gesture, an act of appreciation…a thank you demonstration.

Ahh! thought Haman. *Who would the king wish to honor more than his best officer?* He began parking the rewards in the garage of his own ego.

"What about a purple robe?" Haman suggested. "And the king's own prancing steed? And—oh, yes—the king's royal crown. And a parade!"

Haman's proposal pleased the king. "Yes," he said. He ordered the glad rags, the royal chariot, and the escorts. It was a wonderful idea! Now, would Sir Haman please do all this for the man at the gate who had never been *quid pro quo*-ed for saving the king's life? The king yawned. He was getting drowsy and could do with a long winter's nap.

Sir Haman ate humble pie all the way down main street. He hated the flavor of it. His face turned three shades of red, and he slunk away home, down in the mouth.

His wife said it sounded like bad luck to her. An omen trimmed in black.

About that time, a eunuch appeared to remind Sir Haman that he was overdue for Queen Esther's banquet.

Perhaps he could still fast-talk himself out of purgatory. But this time, the queen spilled the beans. She revealed what Sir Haman planned to do and disrobed his motives, leaving them birthday-bare.

The king turned livid with anger. But before he went into cardiac arrest, a servant suggested using the seventy-five-foot gallows and ready-made noose on the evil plotter. The king seconded the motion.

Haman's bank account was put into Esther's name, but she transferred the assets to her cousin and foster parent, Mordecai. She put him in charge of everything. He became the commander-in-chief.

This seems to be the best place for the last curtain to drop. But there's more.

The law still stood. Esther's people were not home free. She needed letters of cancellation.

The tears on her lovely cheeks melted the king's heart. He told her to write anything she wished, in his name, on his letterhead. He promised to sign it and stamp it with the presidential seal.

The letters went out for overnight delivery. Mail carriers spurred their mules and egged on their camels. The message gave the Jews the right to bear arms—to stand against anyone who tried to harm them. The day that was meant to be D-Day became a Jewish holiday instead, and was celebrated from that year forward.

Today, the king's star still shines on, in history…and in our memories. She was the beauty contestant who knew a wonderful secret about winning:

Just be yourself, and you can't lose.

Deliver me from all prejudice and hate, Father, for these emotions will destroy me. Help me to keep my focus on you, and not on my circumstances. Like Esther, I want to do what is right in your eyes, no matter the consequences. Please help me to make choices that honor you.

Then the LORD God said to the woman
"What is this you have done?"
The woman said,
"The serpent deceived me, and I ate."

Genesis 3:13

Eve

I'M STILL WEARING my sister Eve's hand-me-down genes.

Looking at Eve is like viewing myself in a three-way mirror. Mirrors show everything: front, sides, back; freckles, moles, warts. Worse yet, sometimes I feel like I'm peering into one of those maddening mirrors that magnify everything.

All of us would like to imagine ourselves as attractive. Not as a spare rib or as glorified mud, but as lovely, pretty...maybe even beautiful. However, reality sets in when we look at Eve and see how much we favor her.

We can identify with the hillbilly girl back in "them thar hills" who never owned a mirror. She supposed herself beautiful. One day her Pa went to town and bought her a gilt-edged looking glass. Her reflection told her that she was, in fact, quite ugly. So she dashed the mirror on the rocks, shattering it.

Bashing the glass didn't improve her looks, but we know how she felt. We've all wanted to smash the mirror a few times ourselves.

Eve reminds me of myself. She was influenced by what she heard. I find that same hairline crack reflected in my nature. Like a lot of women, I have a hear-ready ear.

Sometimes I listen to runaway tongues, even if what I hear is turkey bologna instead of one hundred percent beef. I don't ask if it's preshrunk or sanitized. I forget to make everything I hear pass Mom's three-way test: Is it true? Is it kind? Is it necessary?

In order to find out more about myself, I took a closer look at Eve. One day she was walking in her sublime Paradise, when she heard something. It was a new voice. It wasn't God's, or even Adam's. *Whose voice was it?*

When she looked up, she saw the serpent. Did she feel fear? No. The word hadn't even been invented yet.

"Yea," he called out. And Eve started listening. He wouldn't have made first base without a bent and lent ear. He would have struck out.

Next he asked a question.

Eve answered, opening an invitation for further dialogue. The serpent loved it! Snake-handling wasn't her talent, but people-handling *was* his. Now that he had an audience, he could swing in his half-truths and make a home run.

Listening destroyed Eve's innocence and sent her off to a different address. She went from Mrs. Eve, Garden of Eden, Paradise; to Mrs. Adam, East of Flaming Sword Gate, Southwest Asia.

It was Paradise Lost.

Few, if any of us, can listen without letting what we hear affect us in one way or another. And we react to what we are told in different ways. Some of us react outwardly, others inwardly. Eve did a little of both. The inside reactors probably suffer the most damage. A little seed of doubt planted in fertile mind soil yields a fretwork of poisonous ideas.

That Eve-deceiving rascal shows up in our Edens today. We still find ourselves straining to hear what he has to say, and we listen with cat-killing curiosity.

Eve wasn't just influenced by what she heard; she was also affected by what she saw. (Maybe that's why I can't pass a department store window without pining for one of those stylish suits.)

The forbidden Eden tree looked irresistibly pleasant. Haven't we all followed our eyes right smack into trouble? (Maybe we put it on the credit card?)

"I see" + "I want" = "Trouble." It was Eve's formula.

I still see myself in the mirror. I look a lot like my sister.

Eve's genes are cut from a one-size-fits-all pattern. One last painful look that shows that she tried to lay the blame for her actions on somebody else. Ouch!

God saw a fresh set of footprints under the garden's middle tree...Eve's. Then he saw a slither print...guess whose?

He counted the fruit. God knew exactly how much fruit he'd hung on that tree. Missing: one piece.

God knew what had happened even before he found Eve garbed in that ridiculous-looking leafy apron. It was ill-fitting and ugly, and the mismatched fig leaf patchwork was created without a pattern.

God has a way of getting right to the point. His question took no detours.

"What did you do, Eve?"

Eve hedged. She tried to shovel the blame into somebody else's bin. "Uh, the serpent..."

Sound familiar? None of us want to own up to turning out lazy teenagers or throwing the budget into a graveyard spiral by careless spending. No one wants to be blamed for leaving the gas tank of the car on empty.

Eve's fruit-eating binge wasn't worth the calories. She'd had it made. There was no sock-eating washing machine in Eden. No IRS deadline. No one needed insulin-shots or got red eyes from their allergies.

Eve had Paradise and pure communion with God. Then she ate that deadly fruit and shortened her life by several trillion years of earth living. In too short a time, she would be returning to dust. She had trashed God's grand blueprint for her life.

But Eve isn't the Lone Stranger. We've all done it: fumbled the ball so badly we wished God would scrape the chromosomes off our genes and start over.

We've all failed a test or two, but we haven't flunked the final exam yet. Someday God will cover those muddy genes with a beautiful white robe.

Then we can all say, "Bring on the mirror!"

Lord, you know I'm a lot like my sister, Eve. I'm often tempted to do things I know aren't good for me. Give me wisdom to discern good from evil. Help me to trust in your principles. And when I do fall, give me the courage to come to you and admit my failures; not with excuses, but with a repentant heart.

And she said to him, "As surely as you live, my lord, I am the woman who stood here beside you praying to the LORD. I prayed for this child, and the LORD has granted me what I asked of him."

1 Samuel 1:26-27

Hannah

OUR SISTER HANNAH had trouble with "the other woman."

Her husband pulled a double shift of wives. It was a tough job, trying to be fair to each one. There was a delicate balance of equal time, equal rights, and equal allowances. When he winked at one, he had to make sure he winked at the other, otherwise he was in hot water.

This mountain man thought he was juggling things quite well until one of his wives, Peninnah, had a baby boy. That threw the ball way into left field.

Hannah felt left out, neglected. And all the little gifts Elkanah brought her didn't seem to help. He gave her re-assurances and affectionate pats. He whispered sweet nothings into her ear. But none of these things compensated for the ache of emptiness Hannah suffered as she watched the husband she shared play with his Peninnah-born Junior.

Things were bad enough. But then the other woman had another baby. And another. There was a daughter. Then another.

Hannah's apartment was still empty-cribbed. It echoed with bitter silence. No toddler's gibberish could be heard. There were no rompers on the clothesline, no knotted shoestrings to untangle.

Her resentment became malignant. It seemed that whenever she and Elkanah would get seated in her cozy kitchen for a cup of coffee and a chat, there would come a message from Peninnah:

"One of the kids is sick."

"I need help with a discipline problem."

"Have you forgotten that it's Junior's birthday? We're having a party."

It was like a joint bank account, with each wife drawing drafts on the same man's time. Only Peninnah always required more. She had more charge accounts. The sick, lonely feeling hit Hannah in the pit of the stomach. Peninnah had more of Elkanah than she did. Peninnah had his children.

The annual vacation to Shiloh—which should have been the highlight of the year—became a dreaded ritual for Hannah. The trip only intensified her inferiority complex. With all of Peninnah's kids running around, Hannah's barrenness was spelled out in capital letters.

She could hear Elkanah whistling as he packed for the trip. His deep-throated laugh rang out as he told the boys stories and tousled their hair. He ponied the children around on his broad shoulders and drew them maps in the dirt, whetting their excitement for the trip. Elkanah loved his children. He was proud of them. And it showed.

As the years went by, Peninnah's jibes grew nastier, more hurtful. It wore Hannah down. She lost her appetite and cried too much.

One day, they all ate out, but Hannah didn't touch her plate. Elkanah noticed. Something was wrong. It was food she'd always enjoyed. Was she ill?

"What's the matter, Hannah?" he whispered.

The tears that threatened to drown her heart now rose to her eyes, spilling out as she spoke.

"Why do I have to be so lonely?" she cried. "Peninnah has it all. A full heart, full hands, a full life...happiness."

"Am I not better to you than ten sons?"

That was beside the point, but it was all her husband knew to say.

Hannah got up and left the table. Someone else could eat her lamb chop. Enough was enough. She'd taken all she could take.

Finally, bitterness took over. The dam of her emotions broke as she began to sob...and sob...and sob. She'd been forgotten by God. He had left her out of motherhood and denied her the joys of productivity.

Hannah went to the temple. Her lips mouthed her silent plea, offering a prayer...a promise that seemed itself a paradox. She pledged to give back what she wanted when she got it.

The eagle-eyed priest was watching Hannah. His job description included keeping order in the temple, and he couldn't help but notice the woman. After all, she was moving her lips, but not making a sound. *She must be drunk.*

In a way she was. Drunk with desperation. Drunk with sorrow. Drunk with years of dashed hopes.

Eli called her to reckoning and scolded her for drinking too much. It was against the rules. Hannah explained and implored him to leave her out of the barmaid count.

Once he understood, he did a one-eighty and gave her the hope she'd long sought. Eli told her she would never have to wish on a star again. Whatever she craved, that dream would come true.

From that moment on, Hannah was a different woman. She went back to the dinner table and ate everything on the menu, including dessert. Her face glowed as she laughed and talked.

Her husband noticed and gave her a thumbs-up smile. The other woman noticed, too...and frowned.

Their vacation ended on a high note for Hannah. She could hardly wait to get home, to crochet booties, make crib blankets, and knit sweaters—all in blue. Her mother's intuition told her she would have a boy, and that he'd be hale and hearty. She had no ultrasound, no heartbeat monitor, no prenatal vitamins.

She thumbed through books of names but didn't like any of the names she found. Nothing sounded right—until "Samuel," the word meaning "asked of God." After her son's birth, Hannah fulfilled her promise, bringing young Samuel to the house of the Lord in Shiloh to minister under Eli the priest.

The next time she went on vacation, Hannah returned to the exact spot where she'd won her battle. Her one grief-soaked verse was replaced with ten victory verses—verses that spilled out on the pages of a book named in honor of her son.

You see, if you wait long enough, life has a way of evening the score. Hannah was living proof.

And her blessings came out ten to one.

Lord, grant me patience! Small irritations sometimes become a mountain for me, and big problems almost overwhelm me. Remind me to bring my problems to you, like Hannah did, no matter how big or small. And help me to wait patiently for your answers.

She went out and said to her mother,
"What shall I ask for?"
"The head of John the Baptist, " she answered.

Mark 6:24

Herodias's Daughter

❧

LIFE IN A palace isn't always a bed of roses. Just ask the daughter of Herodias.

Roman history remembers her as Salome. The victim of a broken home, she was dominated by her mother and caught in the middle of her parents' breakup.

Herodias had climbed the rungs of the social ladder until she finally reached her desired perch: right in the castle beside King Herod, strutting her stuff. It was her second marriage, and she brought her young daughter with her. She could give the child more advantages than her ex-husband (Herod's brother) could.

Salome felt that pulled-apart sensation divorce brings.

What would life have been like if Mother had stayed with Father? What if there had been no separation? What if Mom hadn't flirted and plotted with Uncle Herod until she and Dad broke up?

The palace children heard scary stories, created from frightening material and black as a year of midnights. It was told that her stepgrandpa once had many innocent babies slaughtered so he could be rid of one poor family's child. It had something to do with Jewish history and some astronomers following a star. They had been headed for Bethlehem, trying to find the newborn King of the Jews, taking him expensive gifts.

Grandpa Herod had asked them to drop back by and let him know when they found the wee King. He had said he'd like to go worship him, too. That was just a ruse, of course, to find out where the child was so that he could have him murdered. The travelers must have known, because they never returned. So Grandpa Herod had every baby under two years old eliminated. That had been a long time ago. Thirty years.

Tales like this made girls like Salome shudder. *Why must grownups be so cruel?*

Stepdad Herod seemed nicer—most of the time, anyway. But he could get angry, too. A leather-girded man named John had gotten in trouble by stepping on the king's conscience. He had looked Herod straight in the eye and told him that he broke the law when he married Herodias, his brother's wife. The rebuke made Salome's stepdad mad, and the forthright man was locked up in jail.

Salome's mom was even angrier than her husband had been, and she hated John from that moment on. She held a grudge against him and nursed a boil of malice. She wanted to kill him, but she couldn't. John had a lot of followers, and her husband was worried about what would happen if John was put to death.

About this time, a big birthday bash was on the agenda for Herod. The invitations to announce the party were created by a calligraphic expert and sent to the hierarchy, the wealthy, and the socialites.

Salome knew what that meant. It would be a real dress-up occasion, calling for coiled hair and starched petticoats. She'd be expected to mind her manners in the presence of adult company. She sometimes felt like a child robot; she'd probably have to perform for the half-drunk crowd. (Her mother hadn't given her dancing lessons for nothing.)

The guests arrived, the band tuned up, and wine goblets tinkled. Everyone was primed for entertainment. The bull fiddle boomed out its beat while the violins sang, and sobbed, and warbled. But the throng wanted more. Herodias took advantage of the moment by presenting her young daughter.

Salome performed her precision steps. She whirled to

the music, curtsied, and wowed the audience. Her stepfather was highly pleased. Mother flashed her a proud smile.

Herod was drunk on the wine of his own self-importance that night. He wanted to show off. So he called the girl to himself and swore before all the lords and captains that, in honor of her Oscar-winning performance, he would give her anything in the world she asked for, even if he had to mortgage half the kingdom.

What should she ask for? An Arabian horse with jeweled saddle? A diamond ring? A new wardrobe?

Salome knew her mother could help with the decision, so she went to ask her advice. It was the convenient set of circumstances Herodias had longed for.

"Ask him for the head of John the Baptist." Her eyes were cold. "Have it brought in on a platter immediately."

The head of man? When I could have any once-in-a-lifetime wish come true? Ugh. What a waste!

But Salome hurried back to her stepdad with her mother's sadistic demand. She knew better than to argue...or disobey. She saw the disappointment on her stepfather's face and knew he was sorry she had chosen such a reward. But surely he had seen her consult with her mother? He must know it wasn't her idea.

Herod had wanted to give Salome something of value,

something that would make an impression on the big shots. But he'd made a sworn promise, and he couldn't chicken out now. The girl must have what she asked for—what she was coerced into requesting.

So the head-chopper was called and sent to the prison cell. A man brought back the head and handed it directly to Salome.

She didn't want it. Poor Salome probably turned pale. She quickly passed it on to her mother, who *did* want it. She'd wanted it for a long time, and she was enjoying the sweet revenge.

Perhaps Salome suffered from recurring nightmares of a bodiless head, never quite understanding why the night she danced so beautifully had ended in so much ugliness.

How does the old adage go? Like mother, like daughter. But it would have been more honorable for Salome to try filling the sandals of the truth-telling dead man than the fancy slippers of her mother.

Father, look past the outside of me to the wounds inside. Help me to forgive those who have hurt me. Be my source of strength, Lord. Let me turn to you for wisdom when circumstances are beyond my control. And teach me to be a follower of all that is true and good.

Then Jehu went to Jezreel.
When Jezebel heard about it,
she painted her eyes, arranged her hair
and looked out of a window.

2 Kings 9:30

Jezebel

IN JEZEBEL, we had one proud and prancy sister.

She would gob on her makeup and flounce out of her bedroom, giving the impression she didn't care who was watching her, just so long as *somebody* was.

Jezebel had to have the best. She insisted on name-brand riding boots, name-brand deodorant, name-brand clothes...even a name-brand husband. Only those who admired a snob would have found her attractive.

She *was* unique. Not many people would ignore a "Beware of Dog" sign. But Jezebel did. When God sent a direct-delivery message by the prophet Elijah, she didn't even blink an eye. The note said if she didn't change her ways, she'd end up as dog food. Unbelievably, the threat of becoming a Gaines Burger didn't faze Jezebel. Her bumper sticker could have read: 1-800-WHO-CARES?

From the minute she set foot in the palace as King Ahab's bride, she began a twenty-seven-year wrestling match with two rulers: an earthly king and a heavenly King. She was pure poison to God's family. What she didn't like, she tried to destroy, including God's prophets, God's altars, and God's plans.

Jezebel provides God's best object lesson of what a lady ought not to be. The very hiss of her name leaves us feeling that a serpent has slithered by.

You may remember the story. Jezebel's husband, Ahab, saw a nice little plot of ground within walking distance of his house and decided he wanted it for an herb garden. He said he wanted it to plant parsley, garlic, and oregano. (Perhaps he liked pizza.)

Ahab tried to finagle the owner, one Mr. Naboth, out of it. But Mr. Naboth said he wasn't interested in selling. Or leasing. Or trading. The property had been in his family for ages. It had sentimental—not monetary—value, and there was some religious ordinance bound up in the deed of trust. This stick-in-the-mud neighbor said he planned to pass the land on to his children. It would never go on the market.

Ahab threw a childish fit. He couldn't have his toy, so he pouted. When he didn't show up for supper, Jezebel sent out a search party for him. Her husband was found in a state of black depression, lying on the bed in his bedroom and acting the part of a colicky infant.

Jezebel went to humor her cry-baby husband. She wanted to know the reason for his rainstorm, so Ahab blubbered out his tear-jerking story.

His wife hooted at him for being such a wimp. "Get up and eat. Be happy!" she demanded. "The very idea of letting such a petty thing bother you! If you're not man enough to get that vineyard, then *I'll* get it for you!" She sashayed out of the room.

While her milksop of a husband shook off his emotional hangover, Jezebel set up a diabolical plot to have an honest man murdered. She employed forgery, false witnesses and perjury. And as always, she got what she went after. The real estate was now her husband's: lock, stock and barrel.

Ahab took a walk in the dead man's arbor, mapping out his future vegetable patch. *Let's see…marjoram here. Cumin there.*

Suddenly a face appeared: a face that had been AWOL for seven years. It was Elijah, the archenemy of Ahab's god, Baal. Elijah knew what Ahab and Jezebel had done, and he warned Ahab that they would suffer for it.

"Tell your wife that the dogs will eat her right here at her crime scene," he said.

The threat did not intimidate Jezebel. *Dogs eat a queen? Ha! That balmy old man is just nursing a grudge. He doesn't know what he's talking about.* She plunged on, headstrong.

Hating God and embracing Baal.

Five years...ten years...fifteen years passed. God set aside a decade and a half for one woman to repent.

She didn't.

Maybe Ahab thought God had lost his wife's address. God hadn't. He had her zip code, too. He knew exactly where she was.

God appointed a man named Jehu to start the blocks toppling. He was the Indy racer of his day, the man who drove his chariot "furiously." The man who cheered for right and booed for wrong. God appointed him king of Israel and ordered him to destroy the house of Ahab.

Jezebel heard through the grapevine that Jehu was in town. She looked out an upstairs window, undaunted. She was used to wowing men. She loved it. So she put on a fresh coat of face paint, fixed a picture-perfect coiffure, and chose her most alluring outfit.

Had she known anything about Jehovah, though, she would have understood that paint and powder couldn't camouflage her inner ugliness. She would have realized that he took inventory of souls, not cosmetic cases.

Repentance would have made a difference. Sackcloth and ashes might have covered her sin. But a haughty spirit was bound to fail.

"Throw her down!" Jehu yelled up. The men closed in behind Jezebel and lifted her for the toss. In the end, vanity put her by the window and delivered the final blow.

"What do you think you're doing? I'm the Queeee—!"

Down she went, over the wall, falling under the hooves of Jehu's horses. That night, at his celebration banquet, he spoke up. "Go see the cursed woman. And bury her." But all the FBI found were pieces: a skull, two feet....two hands.

She lived for the highest of highs. Her death was the lowest of lows.

In the dictionary, our proud sister's name appears as a synonym for a wicked, shameless woman. Not a very pleasant way to be remembered, is it? But it *is* good for us to remember her. Because each of us has a little of Jezebel's attitude. A little of her spirit. A little of her pride.

We all need to "Beware of Jezebel.

Set me free from pride, Lord. Pride will make me follow my own path instead of yours. It will bring me to destruction as surely as it did my sister, Jezebel. So rescue me from my own selfish longings, and clothe me with your humility and righteousness. For I want to serve you, not myself.

I have been reminded of your sincere faith,
which first lived in your grandmother Lois
and in your mother Eunice, and
I am persuaded, now lives in you also.

2 Timothy 1:5

Lois

CONGRATULATIONS, LOIS! You're the only grand-mother to be mentioned in the Bible.

That's quite an honor.

Lois must have had a cookie jar. A brag book. A toy box. Maybe even a mug that said, "Happiness is being a Grandma."

Her daughter Eunice was mixed up in one of those unfortunate marriages—you know, the kind that always brings problems. She had married an unfit man who didn't share her ideals, and her son was spiritually fatherless.

Grandmothers see a lot, but usually say very little.

Surely Lois grieved for little Timothy's lack of male guidance. No doubt she took him into her lap and spent endless hours telling him stories of his maternal ancestors: how they crossed the Red Sea, how God gave Moses tables of stone containing the Commandments, and how each tribe inherited their portions in Canaan.

She must have whispered all the old favorites into her grandson's eager ears: David and Goliath, Samson, King Solomon, the three flame-resistant Hebrew boys, Daniel's night with lockjawed lions.

Lois had more odds to overcome than most. She couldn't take Timothy to all the synagogue functions because the neighbors knew his background. He would be discriminated against because his father was an uncircumcised unbeliever.

But Lois left no stone unturned in the boy's training. She tried hard to pass genuine faith on to him, then trusted God to do the rest.

And he did. God sent Apostle Paul to Granny Lois's hometown, and he became Timothy's spiritual father. There is no question who was the most thrilled when the dynamic preacher called Timothy "my son." Grandmother Lois must have had goose bumps and a swollen heart.

"Timothy," Paul said, "you've known the Holy Scriptures all your life. It began way back at your grandmother's knee."

Lois didn't exert all that effort on her grandchild just to get her name in the Bible. She had no idea that we'd remember her centuries later. All she wanted was to see her grandson saved. She never dreamed that he would become a great preacher and have two books of the Bible addressed to him.

Few people have the patience of godly grandmothers. With knowing smiles, they let those of us in the microwave culture rush on by. "If you don't help me in a hurry, God, I'll have to do it myself," they hear us say. We approach the Father as if we're in an express lane: "I have ten items or less on my request list this morning, so run me through quickly. I have no time to wait."

Years of experience grant grandmothers the wisdom and maturity younger mothers have yet to gain. Every child needs a grandparent with the same noncounterfeit faith that Lois had—someone who can lead a child by example and point him to proper role models.

Many of us can think of at least one such grandparent, silver-haired with age, walking into the sanctuary with a spiritually orphaned grandchild. The worn hand takes that of the small hand. The grandparent bridges the gap, giving the child the advantage of knowing God. A book of success stories could be written in honor of these grandparents.

Time with a grandchild is never wasted.

Lord, please give me an opportunity to influence a child's life. Help my love for you to be contagious, to draw others to you. And may the words I say, and the love I give, plant seeds of faith in the hearts of children around me.

But Lot's wife looked back,
and she became a pillar of salt.

Genesis 19:26

Lot's Wife

LOT'S WIFE was an addict. Addictions come wrapped in different packages: drugs, alcohol, nicotine. This woman was addicted to *things*.

Mrs. Lot didn't use up much of the Bible's ink. All we have to siphon from is a tiny biography in the Old Testament and a three word epitaph in the New. But a few lines is enough to let us know that she was affected by worldly possessions.

She loved the boutiques in Sodom's mall. She loved the whir and buzz of city life: the frenzied activities, eating and drinking, playing and partying. She even liked the business antonyms: buying and selling, building and wrecking, coming and going.

Her background is hazy, but we can guess that she was reared in Sodom, probably educated there. She may even have been on the girl's basketball team or voted "Most Likely to Succeed." Maybe she was the most popular. Perhaps the class secretary.

Whatever the case, when a new gent named Lot came to town, she batted her eyelashes double-time. It was rumored that he had a rich uncle and was quite well-off in his own right. The news tugged at her purse strings.

Lot didn't disappoint her. He got himself elected to the city council and sat with the mayor at the gate. His name was in the tabloids often, and he received a lot of hat-tipping.

But we wonder if he was slowly dying from the cancer of spiritual negligence. Was his soul sick for his uncle's altars, so out of style in the sin-drenched city?

At first, he must have felt out of place. He was a misfit in the wild metropolitan network, uncomfortable with its modes and customs. It was like walking from the bright light of day into a room of total darkness.

That was at first. But apparently, his wife rearranged his priorities rather quickly. She knew if she could keep him in the shadows long enough, his eyes would become accustomed to the dark.

Eventually, Lot became quite at ease. He hardly realized the disadvantages of wickedness and remembered less and less of his Uncle Abraham's pure-water lifestyle.

Sodom once had been outside his heart, but now it had begun to move inside. Like a small animal hypnotized by the slow-moving serpent, he would soon be swallowed whole without a squawk.

Children were born to Mr. and Mrs. Lot. They were all daughters. Lot would have preferred a son or two, but Mrs. Lot was pleased. Her girls became an extension of herself. They grew up, dated boys their type, and lived for the here and now.

When it was time for marriage, the girls chose men untainted by religious phobias. Finally all but two of them were settled into their own godless Sodom homes with their materialistic mother's approval.

Lot's wife sat back, marinated in her pleasant present, and watched her daughters mesh with the ghastly sins about them. Not once did she lift her voice in protest.

Countdown time came for Sodom and her sister city, Gomorrah. God could stomach their sins no longer. The population at large couldn't think a decent thought, and all the good people were buried in the graveyard. Respect was a forgotten commodity.

Three angels with a two-fold mission checked their aeronautical map for the proper airstrip and throttled down to the earthlings' accommodations.

First they went to Uncle Abraham. They had a bit of cheerful news for him. At one hundred years old, he would be waiting outside the delivery room for the cries of a newborn son.

The angels got up to leave Abraham, cutting their eyes toward Sodom, their next assignment. They started to bid the old fellow *adieu.*

But the Lord didn't want to keep secrets from Abraham. The idea went against his grain. After all, this man would father a great and mighty nation. He was one of those pearl-handled men who would shoot straight with his children and teach them to do justice and judgment.

So God showed Abraham his diagram of plans from heaven's drawing board. According to the format, Sodom was to be turned into ashes. This meant Abraham's nephew Lot would lose everything he had.

The angels left, but Abraham stayed with God. He reasoned. He bargained. He even tried to put God on a guilt trip.

Would a just God destroy the good with the bad? That didn't seem like the fair deity God was. One didn't throw out the baby with the bath water. Couldn't the city be saved if fifty good citizens could be found there?

"Yes," God said.

How about forty-five?

"Yes," God said.

Or even forty?

"Yes."

Then maybe he would come down to thirty?

"Yes."

Would twenty do?

"Yes."

One last try. Could he possibly spare the city for ten?

"Yes," God said. He'd see if there were that many.

But there weren't ten respectable townsfolk within the whole perimeter of Sodom. The angels found out the hard way. When they went to visit Lot at his house, they almost got assaulted. They even had to yank Lot in and shut the door to keep him from injury. Then they zapped the unruly bunch outside with blindness to keep them from splintering the door and taking over the house.

The angels had seen enough. They told Lot to get his kith and kin out of the place or else their verdict would be the death penalty, too.

Poor Lot tried—without Mrs. Lot's cooperation. He hurried to his sons-in-law and his married daughters. He relayed the angels' message and urged them to hurry.

But they turned it into a big joke and poked fun at him. The old man was predicting the future as a hobby, they said. He was telling of the end of Sodom and reading horror-scopes. Ha, ha. He should submit his predictions to the Sunday funnies.

The next morning, the angels got hypertonic and tried to put the rush on the parking Lot. He dallied. He got his Walkman stuck on pause. Mrs. Lot puttered around, not wanting to go outside. The single daughters lounged about, unwilling to help pack.

If it's possible for angels to lose patience, these did. They snapped at Lot, "Get up and get going or you will be burned to a crisp with the rest of the no-accounts around here!"

Still he stalled. He refused to push the fast-forward button. So they grabbed his hand. They grabbed Mrs. Lot's hand. And they grabbed the hands of the two youngest girls. The angels yanked them out of the city and set them down for a talk.

"Now run, and don't you dare look back," they said. "Get to those mountains yonder as fast as your legs can carry you, or you're all dead." The tardy bell rang.

"No! No! Not the mountains!" Lot begged. The thought of three women in the wilderness terrorized him…it gave him a choking sensation. Mrs. Lot hated isolated places. His daughters couldn't stand to be so far from civilization. They would be afraid of wild animals.

They couldn't tolerate a life without conveniences. They wouldn't know how to rough it.

Couldn't they go to the small community nearby? It was tiny, but at least there were people. Oh, please? These women of his had to *live*.

"All right," God said. He would exclude the little town from destruction. But the family had to get a move on. God was holding the fireballs mid-ionosphere until Lot vacated the Sodom area.

At sunup the Lord turned loose his brimstone arsenal. Flashes of fire cut a berserk pattern across the early morning sky. The angels helicoptered out before their wings were singed.

Mrs. Lot's body went along with her husband and daughters, but her heart stayed behind, with her other children, with her possessions…with her beloved city.

She partnered in her husband's flight, but not his faith. She felt the heat and heard the rumble. She just couldn't resist a look.

Suddenly, her soft, fleshly hand turned into a stony salt hand. She was a statue; a monument to materialism. Lot's wife became a shrine of unbelief.

If Lot was holding her hand, he probably dropped it and ran. What had his wife, now a lifeless mannequin, wanted from the burning inferno? A jewel? A portrait? A favorite dish? Or did she just want one more quick look at the past to which she was so addicted?

The moral of Mrs. Lot's story can be summarized in three words: Don't look back. Not to forgotten yesterdays, to might-have-beens, or to worldly losses.

Never look back.

God, help me be free from my addiction to things. May I never grasp anything so tightly that I wouldn't willingly leave it behind if you asked it of me. Teach me to know the difference between the trivial and the truly important things in life. And help me to keep my eyes focused not on the world, but on you.

"Therefore, I tell you,
her many sins have been forgiven—
for she loved much.
But he who has been forgiven
little loves little."

Luke 7:47

Luke's Lady

THE LUKE 7 LADY'S reputation was in the red, and some thought her heart was in the black.

Most people would have begrudged her the label of "lady." Her resume didn't include a Sunday school class or Paul's example of the believer. She didn't even have good morals.

But her antagonists made a monumental mistake when they took her at face value. They couldn't see the quality lumber beneath the dingy wallpaper. They missed the timbers of thoughtfulness, her kind spirit and generosity.

She heard that a great Teacher was coming to town. It was said that he had a soft spot for children. The poor. The castaways. The sick. Lepers. The spokes of her circle claimed it was all rumor. But a hyper-thirst made her want to see and hear the man. Unfortunately, he moved around from place to place, and she seemed to always miss him.

Then she heard about the dinner invitation. He was to be a guest at Simon's big fete. *Simon*. The man was bloated with self-righteousness. He was a Pharisee in soul, mind, and attitude.

Our sister knew her name wouldn't be included on the guest list. It wouldn't even come up for nomination. She was a nobody. A nothing. A sinner.

But she *had* to see the Teacher. It became her fixation. She grasped her dearest possession, a flask of expensive perfume, and skirted Simon's house. There, she slipped past the welcoming committee and the guest book, hoping that no one recognized her.

Spotting the Teacher was no problem. She saw him as soon as she entered the room. Something called to her heart, pulling her down the wall to an unobtrusive place behind him. She was so vile, but he was so *pure*.

Standing that near to him, something broke within her. Emotions gone flat had been stored in the old wineskin of her heart. But now it burst open, spilling out her memories of remorse and regret.

She came to her senses as she was weeping and kissing his feet. She had nothing to wipe away the tears that left his skin wet, so she used her hair for a towel. Then she broke the seal on her costly perfume and poured it on his feet.

The smell drowned out the aroma of food and set off Simon's smoke alarm. The Pharisee snapped to attention and scowled at her.

This Teacher doesn't know his P's and Q's. His ESP's not working. He's no prophet. If he was, he wouldn't let that floozy touch him. Simon didn't know he was up against a mind reader.

"Simon," Jesus said, "I need to have a little talk with you."

"Say on," the host flipped. Now was as good a time as any to find out if the man was fake or fact.

Jesus cited an incident that involved two men with similar problems. It seems these two men were beholden to the same banker: one owed a mini-debt, the other a maxi-debt. But when the payment deadline came, both men were broke. They couldn't even pay the interest for another year. There were no rich relatives could bail them out, so the banker (a sympathetic chap) stamped "canceled" across each debtor's bank note.

"Now," asked the Teacher, "Which is apt to love the creditor the most? Who will be the most grateful—feel the most relieved?"

It was elementary. The one who owed the megabucks had the most to gain.

But what did this have to do with anything? Was Jesus trying to throw Simon off the scent of the bad woman?

Jesus turned to look at her and suggested that the Pharisee do the same. As the host, Simon should have offered Jesus the customary courtesies: a basin of water, oil for a travel-weary head, a greeting kiss. The master of ceremonies had been both negligent and rude. Yet the disreputable woman had done all the things Simon should have done, with no resources save that of her own passion.

Yes, the woman had many sins. She'd made a multitude of mistakes and fueled backstairs gossip. But now, all was forgiven. And, like the men in the story, those forgiven much were the ones who loved much.

Simon's friends censured Jesus. *The very idea! What right does he have to erase such a debt?*

"Go in peace," Jesus said to the woman. They were the most liberating words she had ever heard. Gone was the guilt. There was no more need for cover-ups or secrecy. There was no more disgrace or shame beside her name.

The sister who once had no morals, now has a moral for us. For we never fall too low for the Master to lift us. Our failures are his chances to show the world what pardon is all about, to demonstrate his sea of forgetfulness. God doesn't point an accusing finger, but extends a helping hand. He'll even take your smeared page and give you a clean one.

Just have faith in him...and in yourself.

Help me, Lord, not to condemn anyone who has fallen. Strip me of any self-righteousness. Let me not be judgmental. And help me to lift those who have fallen, just as you have lifted me.

"Martha, Martha," the Lord answered,
"you are worried and upset about many things,
but only one thing is needed.
Mary has chosen what is better, and it will not be
taken away from her."

Luke 10:41-42

Martha

MARTHA. MOST OF US know her story all too well.

One day, Jesus dropped in for a visit to one of his favorite spots, Martha's house. There her sister Mary sat eagerly at his feet, while Martha pulled a shift in the kitchen patrol.

Special guests meant extra work for Martha. She set out dinner plates, folded napkins, and filled glasses. While Mary washed Jesus' feet, Martha washed dishes. *Someone has to be practical! If everyone loses their heads in the clouds, we'll all starve to death.*

Mary's priority was hearing what Jesus had to say. She considered food for the soul more important than food for the body. Meals come and go, and we hunger again. But Mary chose something that would last past dinner.

Martha complained that Mary was trying to shirk

her womanly responsibilities. She figured there would be a chance to hear Jesus later, after the serving was through, the soup bowls were dried, and the cracker crumbs were swept up. But she was mistaken.

At the end of the visit, a smile lingered on Mary's face, but Martha's was flushed with fatigue. *It's not fair.* She fought a spasm of resentment. Many things troubled Martha: time, guests, meal preparation. But none of it really mattered. She only needed one thing: communion with God.

Do we need to simplify our lives? We can spread ourselves so thin with our many petty projects that we can begin to resent those who are "not doing their part." The Marys are shirking their duty by not helping us Marthas among the pots and pans. Those who don't meet our measurements are wasting time—theirs *and* ours.

It's easy to fall into the "poor me" syndrome. "I'm doing all the work around here." Feelings of injustice congeal into self-pity. "Nobody *else* takes pizza orders for the church...or scrubs the restrooms...or waters the plants."

Martha carried her piqued emotions to the Master, "Don't you care that my sister has left all the work to me?" But Mary wasn't complaining, "Master, make my sister come and sit with me at your feet. Don't you care that I sit here alone while she makes the gravy?"

Martha made a mistake trying to rope Jesus into taking sides. "Martha, Martha," he answered, "you are worried and upset about many things, but only one thing is needed. Mary has chosen what is better, and it will not be taken away from her."

Jesus didn't dislike practical, methodical Martha. Indeed, he loved her very much and called her name twice, with the utmost tenderness. He gave her the front seat in John's eleventh chapter, ahead of Mary. He didn't even mention Mary's name. The verse says he loved Martha and her sister and Lazarus.

We're all riding on the world-go-round. Some of us are a lot like Martha, some a little more like Mary. God loves each one of us just the way we are. It is only when we become overbalanced with serving and become too encumbered that he has to jerk us back to reality with his "Martha, Martha" leash. Because he loves us so much, he doesn't want us ever to forget the best part.

Martha's lesson? Take time to smell the roses.

Especially the Rose of Sharon.

How like Martha I find myself! Burdened by earth's problems, buried under my daily ritual, I take such little time to sit at your feet. But today, I'll take the time...make the time. I can't afford to forget the "one thing" that is the best part of my existence.

Now Saul's daughter Michal was in love with David,
and when they told Saul about it,
he was pleased.

1 Samuel 18:20

Michal

SOME WOMEN CHOOSE a husband for all the wrong reasons. Michal may well have been one of those women.

She didn't look at the most important things. Michal wasn't interested in the motor, but the chrome. She liked the pin-striping, the boom box.

As a child in the palace, her dress-up-like-a-grownup props would have been royal garage sale items like discarded earrings, jaded crowns, broken scepters and outdated ball gowns. Princesshood was the only life she knew. Her dad was king. He'd been the country's kingpin since she was born.

At sweet sixteen, Michal could pick any of the male kingdomites. She had carte blanche and could invest her vanity wherever she wished. Eeny-Meeny-Miney-Mo.

She had little in common with David. They didn't march to the same music, didn't fly the same flag. The two were plugged in to different frequencies. A computer match-up program would have pled insanity and expired when fed their conflicting data.

Michal was from proud and rebellious stock, and she never conquered her feelings of superiority. Her life was cut from a Vogue pattern. David was a lowly shepherd boy. He wore his humility like a shepherd's coat. His life was scissored from brown paper.

Michal probably inherited her father's volatile temperament, causing her to become angry and ungovernable at the drop of a hat. On the other hand, David was a tender-hearted young man, easily touched by the feelings and needs of others. David was quick to repent and willing to relent. He was the opposite of Michal.

What attracted Michal to this common farm-bred boy? David was good looking and fearless. Maidens whispered about him, ladies swooned. He was a hero who became a knight overnight. When he returned from his victories, women flocked about him in a sort of worship. They sang, danced, and called out his name. (He probably blushed.)

Window watching was one of Michal's favorite pastimes, and she noticed as this handsome shepherd-boy-turned-champion took the heart of the city with him. People followed him like the Pied Piper.

Maybe that's when her infatuation started. It's possible

she didn't realize that the package deal would include some less-than-glamorous moments. She didn't think about the dirty socks, the shirts to iron, or the Jehovah-loving in-laws.

Michal was drawn to the public image she saw out the window. But could she love the all-human man behind the applause and stardom? If David were no longer borne on the shoulders of cheering crowds, how would she feel about him then? Would she have been content to sit peasant-dressed and barefooted beside him on a Judean hill, listening to the harp-accompanied songs flowing unrehearsed from his heart?

Was she willing to stand beside him for better or for worse? Was she ready to face flat tires, dead batteries, and empty gas tanks? Was she willing to take care of him, so he could perform his best?

Saul was insanely jealous of David's fame. He envied the praise David had received when he returned from his giant-slaying tournament, and he eyed David daily with evil intent and watched for opportunities to do him in.

When Saul heard of his youngest daughter's interest in the budding celebrity, he was pleased—for all the wrong reasons. He figured his daughter could snare this popular whippersnapper's devotion. So he put a price on the princess: the slaying of one hundred Philistines. In his attempt to earn the right to marry her, Saul figured, David would become a statistic.

It was easy to justify his actions. A king, Saul decided, shouldn't have to share the attention of his subjects with a backwoods nobody. But the plan didn't work. David turned the tables and won the king's daughter for his wife.

The brave-hero days and the king-crowning days pleased Michal's vanity. But she did not like the bother of David's religion. The temple ceremonies made no sense. She hated watching priests kill animals and observing boring feasts. What David loved the most, Michal despised. Their worlds split off into separate orbits as they grew farther apart.

She hadn't really thought through her choice of a husband. She hadn't looked beyond the shiny hood ornament. She was surprised by the interior fabric and the gear ratio.

Before long, she parked David by the curb of her selfishness. And while David ran from the javelin of Saul, she thumbed a ride with someone else: a man named Paltiel.

We're given no inkling that she missed David. We hear no more from her for the next fourteen years. She was happy in the land of Gallim, away from Jerusalem and the center of worship. She must have meshed quite well with her new surroundings because when David demanded her back, she left behind a sniveling second husband who was reluctant to release her.

Her heart stayed wed to Paltiel. It appears she never loved David after that interim marriage. Bondo couldn't smooth over the dents after the wreck. STP couldn't help the motor. There would be no more joyrides with his dreams, his ambitions or his victories.

If Michal had truly loved David, his greatest dream would have been important to her. He longed to bring the beloved ark of God from the house of Obed-Edom back to its rightful place in the capital city. If she'd loved him, she would have gone with him, at least in spirit. She would have stood beside him, supported him, and encouraged him.

She wouldn't have been expected to play the harp like her skillful, talented husband. But couldn't she have picked up the tambourine as Miriam did and show her allegiance to David's God? Anything to be party to the greatest day her husband had ever known, to feel the breath-taking ecstasy, the all-consuming joy, the soul-stirring awe.

But no. All such liturgy was beneath her self-centered ego. It annoyed her, like a hair in her soup. The more she thought about it, the angrier she became. To think that a square box could mean that much to a man of such high rank! Her father hadn't been this overwrought with religious fervor.

Suddenly, David seemed a foolish sentimentalist to Michal. The chasm between the two widened until David's first love had become the object of Michal's bitter hatred.

When he returned, she watched him out of her

window. Was this the model she had chosen? Stock. Untinted glass. No options. Coated with dust.

She saw the whole procession as obnoxious. The grand hero, David, stopped the parade every six steps to sacrifice oxen and calves. He leapt wildly and danced in a frenzy, all the way up the street to the palace. He was beside himself!

A tumor of hostility had been growing inside Michal for several months, and now it ruptured. How she despised that dancing man! He turned her stomach. Must he flaunt his imbecility in front of everyone? The butcher. The baker. The candlestick maker. Such actions were idiotic!

David's jubilant behavior mortified Michal's pride. She was ashamed to be associated with him in any way, especially through matrimony. He might make a fool of himself, but he would not make a fool of her!

With a scowl on her face, she gathered her arsenal of words and got ready for verbal battle. She prepared to kill the giant of scandal and outrage that preened in the valley below her lookout. Scalding words formed on her tongue. She planned to tell David just what she thought of his embarrassing exhibition.

David came home with the noble intention of blessing everyone, including his household, his servants...and his wife. But before he could open his blessing-ready mouth, the dam of Michal's anger broke and the insults gushed forth.

He'd made a fool of himself, stooped below his royalty, and disgraced his dignified position. She slapped him with scorn again and again.

The lash of unkind words must have shocked David. Surely they hurt him. They probably left his ears and his heart smarting. He could have ordered Michal's vile mouth sealed by instant death. But revenge was not in the woof of David's weave.

Instead he explained his behavior. "What I did was before the Lord." It was as simple as that. And in the future, he said, he would seek and find his honor among the lowly household employees—the praise that should have been his wife's to give.

David left Michal's punishment up to God, and she died a desolate, childless, old woman. She wrote her own disharmony, her own sour notes, on a clef of contempt, when she should have sung with David. She could have been praising the Lord with him on his staff of victory.

But David's last recorded song was a solo.

Lord, I haven't always been the companion I should be. Help me not to let a root of bitterness spring up in my heart. Let my words be without rancor. Make a reverence for you my anchor. And bless my home with unity and peace.

His sister stood at a distance
to see what would happen to him.

Exodus 2:4

Miriam

MIRIAM TOOK HER sisterly responsibilities too seriously. She didn't know when to cling and when to wing.

Jochebed's third pregnancy came at a bad time. The Pharaoh of Egypt was suffering from an insecurity complex. He harbored a phobia that the leaderless, weaponless Hebrew slaves camped in his back forty would get their heads together and have his. So he decided he'd head off that maneuver by a mass massacre of newborn progenitors.

Step One: Exit the womb.

Step Two: Enter the world.

Step Three: Exit the world. That was his law, his inhumane plan.

But Jochebed—and God—had other notions for her fondling. He was too handsome to become crocodile bait. So she hid him for a month. It turned into two months. Then three months. Common sense told her she couldn't keep her secret indefinitely. Some tattletale was bound to squeal.

Jochebed wore her thinking cap threadbare. How could she save her unnamed baby from this insane monarch?

She decided to gamble. Parking her baby in a bulrush basket, Jochebed waded out ankle-deep in the river and left him among the cattails. As she turned away, demons of logic hopscotched between faith's angels. From worry to hope. Back to worry, then prayer. Worry, faith, worry. It was the same order most mothers follow.

This is where big sister Miriam stepped in. Hiding her pigtails among the cattails, she watched over her baby brother like a setting hen. When she heard someone coming, she backslid a few cattails. The princess had come for her sitz bath, but before she had time to unpack the oatmeal soap, she saw the pitch-daubed baby boat.

"Hark!" she commanded. "Fetch."

Her maidens flew to the flags to do her bidding. When she opened the box, the babe kidnapped her heart. She knew he was a Hebrew...one of those forbidden infants on death row. But who was less afraid of the power-bitten king than the princess? Like all daughters, she had her father wrapped around her little finger. If she wanted a real live doll-baby, she'd just pout until papa said yes.

The pigtails emerged from the cattails.

"Miss Pharaoh," Miriam spoke up, "would you like for me to find you a top-notch baby sitter for this child you are adopting? I happen to know a good nurse."

"Go."

It was the biggest little word Miriam had ever heard. And the sweetest. She would have won Saint Paul's race getting to her mother.

From that day on, Miriam took Moses on as her special project, becoming unrelentingly sisterish. Through the years, she traveled from place to place with Moses, always keeping him in sight, refusing to let go. She never married. Brother Moses was enough to occupy her thoughts and blot up her affections.

His first great victory was also hers. It called for a Miriam-engineered rally. She organized a women's choir and orchestra. There were tambourines, dances, and songs.

Her brother had brought the Israelites safely across the Red Sea. Moses. The same baby brother she had diapered, burped, and taught to walk. "Look at him now!"

Miriam didn't care for her sister-in-law. She thought the woman wasn't good enough for Moses, that she didn't understand him like his sister did. She was from a different background. Miriam didn't even like the woman's *name*, Zipporah. Why didn't the hag stay in Ethiopia where she belonged? She certainly didn't fit in the caravan with as perfect a man as Moses! Miriam said it out loud.

111

Moses heard it. The people heard it. God heard it.

And he got ruffled.

God hurried down in a pillar-shaped cloud and blocked the doorway so nobody could come in or go out. Then he had a heart-to-heart talk with Miriam about her brother. She had no right to criticize him for the wife he had chosen, even if she was jealous of the woman's position. She'd crossed God's electric fence.

When God finished speaking, he left a good case of leprosy in Miriam's bloodstream to teach her a lesson about turning her beloved brother over to God. She had to be grounded, suspended.

But Moses couldn't bear to see his overprotective sister suffer. Sure she was a pest sometimes, but aren't all sisters? Moses cried. God couldn't stand the tears of a meek man like Moses, so he expelled Miriam for seven days, then let her go back to class.

Moses stopped the whole Hebrew convoy for that week. Miriam held up the traffic, backing it up from the red light for miles. They all became racy, waiting for the signal to turn green again.

Miriam never said another word about her brother's wife. If she had bad thoughts, she kept them to herself. But she didn't give up. She made sure Moses could see her in his rear-view mirror at all times. When the weary wanderers were turned back into the wilderness for their unbelief, Miriam put on her forty-year guaranteed heels and went right along with her brother.

She didn't keep her shoes on the entire time, though. She only made it through twenty-one years. Then she checked in her traveling bags. For nineteen more years, Moses trudged on without Miriam, his childhood guardian and friend. God knew she couldn't have borne to let Moses go. She had to go first.

Maybe it's best she didn't live to see her brother make the mistake that lost him his acreage in Canaan. She missed the angry outburst and harsh words. They were out of character with the gentle nature she had known and nurtured.

It's museworthy to note that Moses' big flub came after he lost the influence of his big sis. Her smile was gone, along with her advice and encouragement. Moses knew that holding on too tightly was not an unpardonable sin. It was just an idiosyncrasy. He could rest assured that Miriam would be hidden somewhere across chilly Jordan, waiting for him among the golden cattails.

Who knows? Had she stayed around, Miriam might have had the gall to pester Michael about where God had buried her baby brother.

And that was a military secret no one was supposed to know.

Thank you, Lord, for the loved ones in my life. Show me when to give encouragement and support, and when to back away. Let my words and actions build others up, not tear them down. And help me to remember that their lives—and mine—are always in your hands.

The women said to Naomi: "Praise be to the LORD,
who this day has not left you
without a kinsman-redeemer.
May he become famous throughout Israel!
He will renew your life
and sustain you in your old age.
For your daughter-in-law, who loves you
and who is better to you than seven sons,
has given him birth."

Ruth 4:14-15

Naomi

I LIKE OPTICAL illusions.

Take houndstooth for example. First it looks like white checks on black, then it switches to black on white. Or look at the fence posts beside the road. When you start out in your car, the posts seem to be moving while you're standing still. Then the next thing you know, you're moving and they're not.

Naomi's life is like an optical illusion. Sometimes we see her grief against the background of better days. Then we see the good times standing out from the sorrow.

This blushing bride started out with all her eggs in one basket. She had a husband with a good job, hometown property, and friendly neighbors. Her life was filled with laughter and plenty. And added to all this, she had a bouncing baby boy, Mahlon, followed by another, Kilion. Her happiness kept stacking up, multiplying, and snowballing. You can see the white checks in the pattern.

But suddenly the design changes. First, the Great Depression hit. Her husband lost his good-paying job, and their savings were sliced away like pieces of a cake. Elimelech cinched up his belt and ate less so the children could have more. But still, Mahlon came home from school hungry. Kilion lost weight. Naomi used up everything she had canned the year before and went on an unplanned diet.

When their taxes came due, there was no money to pay them. They got cut-off notices on the utilities, and the bills stacked up. Naomi gathered up a few keepsakes, their clothes, what courage she could find, and followed her breadwinner to Moab, a country she didn't like. Starting over from scratch, they lived there among strangers.

Curious residents peeked at the new across-the-border family who carried no gods of wood or stone in their knapsacks. Rumor had it that these outsiders folded up and refused to work the last day of the week. They had ten rules to live by. Their God was an unseen presence. And they didn't eat pork.

The family hadn't been settled long when the unthinkable happened: Naomi's husband died. The taproot of her life was gone. She listened to the last rattle and husk of his breathing and sent for the mortician.

Now she was stuck in Moab. A widow with two children.

Smiles became her greatest expense. Existence was all that mattered. Somehow she managed. It would have been nice for her if her sons could have married someone she knew from back home. Someone of the same religion, the same values, the same culture.

But they didn't.

The boys fell in love with Moabite girls: Orpah and Ruth. Big-hearted, mother-wise Naomi accepted both her daughters-in-law for who they were and what they were. She didn't try to change them or rearrange them. She didn't nag about the way they kept house, their mode of dress, or even their pagan rites.

Ten years blurred by. Naomi followed the hearse twice more to the cemetery, this time escorting the bodies of her two sons to their premature interment, where a mother's duties stop and God's start.

For her tomorrow, there was no husband, no children, and no grandchildren. Desolation camped on Naomi's doorstep. Within her breast lay a heart overweight with tragedy.

This would be the hardest, harshest, most bitter day of her life. It was the day the houndstooth turned to black checks. Nothing worse could happen. Mentally, she closed shutter after shutter behind her.

Meanwhile, a rumor crawled through from her famine-ravaged homeland. It seemed the economy had improved, and the stores were stocking food again. A yearning for returning ate holes in Naomi's mind.

The girls who had once been married to her sons were young and childless. They would find other men to marry; she couldn't fault them for that. She knew they would stay in their country, but she had to return to hers.

When time came for the goodbyes, Ruth couldn't say the word. She had erased it from her vocabulary. She wouldn't let Naomi leave without her. She was a special daughter-in-law, indeed. Church clubs are named for her. Wedding song themes center on her words. Daughters are christened in her honor.

Did Ruth ever have second thoughts about her decision? Did she have anxiety attacks or wonder if she had made the right choice as she went thither to go whither?

Surely she had studied ancient history enough to know that the people of Bethlehem were terribly prejudiced, and not inclined to be friendly to Moabites. An old sore still festered from bygone years. Moabites were considered enemies of Abraham's seed under a ten-generation exclusion clause.

But love bleached out Ruth's fears.

Naomi's relatives had to ask who she was, so tragic was the toll the years had taken on her. Naomi claimed her name didn't fit her anymore. The word meant "pleasant," and was a name that went along with the white checks in the pattern of life. Now that her houndstooth had switched to black, she wanted to be called "Mara." The name meant sad. She had come back empty and afflicted by Providence. Somehow, she had gotten on the wrong side of God.

Ruth landed a job right away, and worked hard in the fields. She helped, toiled, and cared for her mother-in-law. She was young and society-worthy, and no one had asked her to stagnate with an old lady. It was her choice to stay with the woman she loved like a mother.

Ruth's purpose was to sustain herself and her late husband's mother. But God had another purpose in mind: that she meet Mr. Boaz. As the owner of the field where she worked, he was the big boss, and rich. He was also a relative of Naomi.

Ruth's devotion to her mother-in-law traveled from tongue to tongue. Naomi spread some thick compliments herself. With such a special daughter-in-law, who could be expected to staunch a bragging urge?

Someone told Boaz the story, and he liked what he heard. He invited Ruth to lunch with his reapers and filled her cereal bowl himself.

Naomi knew about civics. The law called for the next

of kin to marry young widows of deceased kin, and Boaz was one of the law's closest targets. So before long, according to Naomi's instructions, Ruth almost proposed to the man...leap year or not. But by that time, he was in love and didn't care. With the exchange of a shoe to clear up a legal tangle, Boaz made plans to marry the little Moabite girl.

Ruth went from rags to riches. Her love built a bridge across the wide river of prejudice, taking her from gods who could not hear to the God who always hears.

The tricky illusionary pattern changes again, back to white checks.

As the story ends, Naomi holds a beautiful baby in her aged arms. Rocking and crooning, she smiles a sweet smile. The thunderstorm is over. The air is clear again.

Congratulatory cards come pouring in. "God has blessed you!" a neighbor remarks. "By your daughter-in-law who loves you and is better to you than *seven* sons would have been!" You can almost detect envy in her tone. (Maybe *she* had the seven sons.)

Naomi's friends gathered for a baby-naming party, crowding around her to admire the infant. The name "Obed" won by popular vote, but they nicknamed him "Naomi's son."

She had full arms again, a full heart, and happiness. In the end, it was clear: it isn't really the pattern of life that matters.

It's the fabric.

Father, sometimes I don't understand your plan. I complain that life isn't fair. I forget that you see the whole picture, while I only see a small part of it. Whisper a reminder to me that all my tomorrows must pass by you before they come to me. And in times of trouble, uphold me in your arms as you did Naomi.

She said to the king,
"The report I heard in my own country
about your achievements and your wisdom is true.
But I did not believe these things
until I came and saw with my own eyes…"

1 Kings 10:6-7

The Queen of Sheba

YOU CAN'T BELIEVE everything you hear.

That was the Queen of Sheba's theory. Some people are just like that. They brook no second-hand data. Their favorites words are, "Prove it."

The *Sheba Enquirer* had blown things all out of proportion again. There ought to be a law against it. Each reporter competed with the next ambiguous journalist for the most braggadocio in an article. The protagonist was a king from up north named Solomon.

Can't they find anyone else to write about? With every issue, the stories grew wilder, more ludicrous. Solomon's annual income was (reportedly) twenty million dollars. He had three hundred shields of gold, three pounds of gold per shield. He drank from golden glasses.

Someone called the queen's attention to the account of a roving reporter who professed to have had a personal interview with one of Solomon's staff members. He said the king's throne was overlaid with the best gold in the world. Two carved lions guarded it. And leading to this gold-plated ivory seat were six steps with lions on each side. A full dozen.

There were more flying reports, word-of-mouth exaggerations. He had fourteen hundred chariots. Silver was as plentiful as pebbles on the driveway. A rash rumor had it that the palace dining hall had gardens hanging from the rafters and that peacocks pulled wine carts from table to table. Who could believe such gone-to-seed tales?

But what topped it all, and made the queen know it was a myth, was the part about the wives. Seven hundred wives? No man, hierarchy or no, would be that brave!

When the headlines blared "World's Richest King Goes on Easter-Egg Hunt for Happiness," someone handed Sheba's queen the paper. It said that Solomon had hired the funniest jesters to tell him jokes and mime stories. He wanted them to tumble wildly and make him laugh.

But that didn't work. It was gossiped that Solomon pitched the comedians out, saying everything they did was dumb and stupid. Shallow.

Solomon wrote in his logbook, "Laughter is mad. What does it do for a person?" Then he closed his book to think some more.

He heard that wine cheered people up, so he called for vintage wine, the kingdom's select. It was premium quality.

"Umm. Ish thish good? Shatishfying?" No. It only made him more miserable. It even gave him a headache.

He tried horticulture. Gardens and orchards. Flower beds and vineyards. But he was still unhappy.

How about concerts? Music? Classical. Operatic. Country and Eastern. Orchestras. Bands. Brass. It was all noise that frazzled his nerves and wearied his mind. "Scram, musicians!"

The grapevine reported that Solomon's next step was building pools. Spas. Saunas. A molten sea. Next, he bought cows and horses. He had more cattle than any rancher in Jerusalem. Fresh butter. Whipped cream. Cottage cheese.

Chariots came and went to Egypt like taxicabs. They brought the finest thread available and rare jewels from Arabia, from Tarshish. There were diamonds for Solomon's crown, rubies for his belt buckle, and jade for his saddle.

These treasures didn't seem to impress the king as they should. He scorned them as simply being minerals from the earth, dug from the ground where he would be buried someday.

"King Declares Everything Vanity and Vexation," the headlines read. "King Returns to Fountainhead of Search: Quest for Wisdom and Knowledge."

Professors. Teachers. Philosophers. Educators. Orators.

When all is said and done, the king complained, a wise man dies just like an ignorant one.

The media wouldn't let up. So the queen grabbed her toothbrush, her crimping pins, and her suitcase. She had to check this out. The world's smartest man? One who could answer any question? She didn't believe it.

If it was true, though, she would need to be prepared. She took expensive gifts, just in case. Servants loaded the camel train with spices. They brought out the armored chariot and filled it with gold and other valuables. A whole regiment went along to keep the queen company: she brought guards, chauffeurs, ladies in waiting, and grooms.

Solomon rolled out the red carpet and gave the queen a tour of the palace. What gorgeous clothes his cupbearers wore! And how well-trained they were! They never missed a step. The banquet tables were breathtaking. The *Sheba Enquirer* hadn't told the half of it. An entire issue could have been dedicated to the king's ring.

But the amazing thing was the attitude of the attendants. All of them wore smiles that seemed to be permanently etched in their faces. It was clear, they loved being a servant of this man. Someone whispered that there hadn't been a war since Solomon had become king.

The queen began asking questions. Hard questions, tricky questions, to all the problems she had ever wanted solved. Solomon gave the solutions—just like that. She couldn't find an equation too hard for him, a riddle too tangled.

This was too much. It was all true: everything she had heard and read...and more. The queen swooned and lost her breath. The servants had to fan her. They passed the smelling salts and bathed her face.

A man like this was worthy of everything she had brought: three and one-half million dollars. She gave him exclusive stones and more spices than he'd ever received at one sitting.

As the queen left, Solomon gave her gifts as well. In fact, he gave her anything she asked for, and added an endowment from his royal bounty.

Always investigate for yourself. That was the queen of Sheba's viewpoint, and a good one. It takes away the guesswork. You don't have to take anybody else's word for anything.

It pays to check out the facts.

It's easy for me to take things for granted, Lord. Give me a searching mind and a seeking heart. I want to see and know for myself what you are really like. Please make me willing to do all I can to learn more about you.

Isaac, who had a taste for wild game, loved Esau,
but Rebekah loved Jacob.

Genesis 25:28

Rebekah

REBEKAH CAN TEACH you how to do long division in one easy step. I beg your pardon. Make that one easy *mis*-step.

Her tale is the Bible's sweetest love story and she is our favorite bride. No lass was so fetching as she at the well, watering ten thirsty camels for Abraham's oldest servant.

She didn't do the good deed to gain Brownie points for herself. She didn't even know there had been a peculiar prayer, or that there was a reward for the most willing camel-waterer in Mesopotamia. It was just her way. She was courteous and natural. Faithful. She went beyond the call of duty.

When the servant explained the sweepstakes and asked Rebekah if she would accept the winnings, she didn't hesitate. She would become Isaac's one and only: a monogamous marriage, a rare blessing in her era.

For almost twenty years, Rebekah and Isaac enjoyed a blissful relationship. She comforted him in the loss of his mother, inherited her mother-in-law's home, and redecorated. They lived by a beautiful and historic well.

Then somewhere between Chapter 24 and Chapter 27 came the long division problem. Isaac sent a special request to heaven for children, and back came the answer.

Rebekah sensed the struggle even before her twins were born. When the soft bubble of new life graduated to a wild thrashing within her, she ran to God for an explanation.

S.O.S.!

There were two warring nations cooped up in one womb, God said. Jacob and Esau were as different as salt and pepper. They were born to divide husband and wife.

Rebekah's preference showed: Jacob.

So did Isaac's: Esau.

The words, "Isaac...loved Esau, but Rebekah loved Jacob" rip apart the myth-natured love story. We see two hearts divorce as the romance fades from a once-perfect union.

Because of her favored son, Rebekah began to connive against her husband. Her love for the boy outweighed her love for Isaac. Jacob became her passion. What he itched for, she scratched to get for him, heedless of wounds, pains, and scars.

She was a foolish woman. Placing allegiance with a child against a companion can only tear down a home. A house divided cannot stand; it faces certain collapse.

Wise women build, using their bonding powers to keep the family unit intact. They cement it together with harmony, welding each member to the others in order to strengthen the whole structure. They use the Super Glue of prudence.

Jacob wanted to be the spiritual leader, even though Esau had been born first, and Rebekah agreed that Jacob was more qualified for the job. Esau was a rough, rugged venison hunter. He was too wild and impulsive. Too irresponsible. But Jacob's shoes were precisely the right size to be the leader. So she helped him deceive his father.

Birthright blessing time neared. Isaac had celebrated his 137th birthday and was going blind. He feared death would surprise him some day soon. It was time to turn the reins over to Esau.

Rebekah heard Isaac send Esau to the woods to hunt deer. The old gentleman would eat the meat before conferring the blessing. Something had to be done at once or Esau would be sworn in. Shrewdly, Rebekah set about to divert the blessing to the son she considered the most blessing-worthy.

Through schemes and dishonesty, she devised a way to turn the river of birthright bounty from Esau to Jacob. She knew her poor aged husband could hardly squint past the end of his nose, so she garbed Jacob in Esau's smelly hunting clothes. She put fur on his arms to make him seem hairy like Esau. Then she camouflaged a couple of goats to taste like elk and sent Jacob to get Esau's blessing by theft.

The cost of the birthright for Jacob was three lies:

Lie One: He said he was Esau.

Lie Two: He said he had done what his father had asked.

Lie Three: He said the meat was venison.

A fake name, a fake answer, and fake food. All to please his mother.

Surely this isn't the same Rebekah we met at the well? Termites of division had eaten at the peg of her marriage until the beautiful picture fell from the wall, damaged beyond repair.

Mothers can undermine a father's authority in small ways:

"Don't tell your father I let you drive the car today."

"Don't mention to Dad that I put this sweater on the charge account."

"Don't let your papa find out you made the long distance call."

Neither Rebekah nor Jacob had many happy moments after the betrayal. Side effects kept cropping up. The medicine that cured the headache damaged the heart.

Rebekah said she was willing to take the consequences for the deception she had engineered, and she did. Reaping comes after planting. Payback after buying on credit. Heartaches after deceit.

Hearing that the irate Esau planned to kill his twin brother, Rebekah shipped Jacob off into exile. Hopefully, she took a good long look at her pride and joy before he left for Paddan Aram, because she would never see him again.

Rebekah was left a heartbroken old woman, vexed by Esau's heathen wives. She finished out life with a disappointed husband. And when Jacob returned twenty years later, Rebekah lay beside her mother-in-law in Machpelah's cemetery.

If that one verse could have been deleted from the Bible—the verse that tells of a mother's favoritism—how might things have turned out? Life without the problem of long division and its remainders.

Perhaps we'll never know.

Through Rebekah's lesson, I am made aware of how easily a rift can be made in the closest of family units. May I never be a party to division, Lord. May I never show favoritism. And may I always seek to strengthen my relationships with others—and with you.

...From the beginning of the harvest
till the rain poured down from the heavens
on the bodies,
she did not let the birds of the air touch them by day
or the wild animals by night.

2 Samuel 21:10

Rizpah

RIZPAH KNEW ABOUT crooked politics. She knew too much for comfort.

Whenever a new king took over, he cleaned house. The sweep usually meant getting rid of all the human dust from the old systems. The process killed off any possible rivals, sent heirs into hiding, and eliminated the families of competitors. It was downright frightening.

Rizpah had been connected with King Saul. She was in his harem. His call girl, a concubine. She had two sons fathered by Saul, and they were in line to pay the penalty for the wrongdoings of a bloodthirsty leader.

The Gibeonites had been promised government asylum in Israel, but Saul had broken the pact and killed some of them. Now the debt had been passed on to the next king.

Saul's silver and gold wouldn't suffice to pay the debt, nor would any treasures from his house. The Gibeonites wanted seven of Saul's sons in repayment. The lives of Rizpah's children were on the line, along with those of five other descendants of the suicide-doffed king.

Barley harvest had barely started when her sons were sentenced to death by hanging. Time stopped for Rizpah. She was surrounded by rich fields of golden grain, a big harvest moon, and chattering reapers. But Rizpah saw none of them.

How can the world go on? How can the sun come up shining? How can laughter ring out across the meadows when my sons swing from a rope, limp and lifeless? Dead they might be, but Rizpah could not bring herself to walk away and leave their decaying bodies to the birds of prey by day, beasts by night.

So she took a piece of sackcloth, spread it on a rock nearby, and camped there with no intentions of leaving. No buzzard would pick the flesh from the bones of her sons!

Only a mother could empathize with the heart-pain Rizpah experienced. Dry, hot days merged into long, sleepless nights. She endured tortuous, mind-breaking hours. Thirty timeless days and nights passed while the unsympathetic rock dug into her joints and bruised her flesh.

Rizpah ignored the aching muscles and the sickening smell. She fought away the wretched gagging. She forced down just enough food to stay alive, and she stayed alive just to ward off predators.

Rizpah could have left anytime. She could have taken her pallet and gone home. But that would have been useless. For when she closed her eyes in her comfortable bed, she would have had nightmares of big, black birds tearing at the framework of her sons. She would hear the howl of a distant wolf fighting for the skeletal remains in the tree.

Another thirty days went by, and the nights chilled around the edges. Rizpah's head ached from broken sleep. Did her hot forehead indicate fever? Was she becoming ill? She couldn't! She had to have strength to shoo away the varmints. But winter was coming. What then?

From the beginning of harvest until the rains started—at least three months time—Rizpah kept her outdoor vigil. How long she would have stayed, no one knows.

Finally, someone reported her to King David. He was told of her loyalty and how she was wasting away on the rock. David knew grief for a dead son. He'd been there himself. He was easily touched by tenderhearted accounts such as this.

He ordered that the bones of Rizpah's sons be taken down and given a proper burial. It was a small gesture on his part, but a great favor to a hurting mother. Rizpah couldn't call her two sons back, but when she picked up her bedspread and went home, she had the satisfaction of knowing that their bones were now safe. She could sleep without nightmares.

God used a unique pattern when he was scissoring out mothers. He gave them a gift no other creature has. Like timeworn clocks, the inner mechanisms keep ticking. Even after the face is cracked and the hands are worn, one mainspring of hope outlives all other working parts, and these amazing wonders of creation know when it's time to pray.

Some biological mothers are made of plastic, like Barbie dolls. Some are mothers in name only. But mothers like Rizpah are real. Often, they are called to stand guard over children's souls...even adult children who seem past help, dead in trespasses and sin. These mothers chase away evils that would pluck at the spiritual sinews of their offspring. They keep their vigil until the King of kings takes notice, and the rain falls from heaven.

Day after day, these mothers never give up.

Dear God, I could use more perseverance today. I give up more easily than my sister Rizpah did. When I call you, I hang up if you don't answer on the first ring. Correct this flaw in me. Repair my mainspring of hope so that I'll keep believing, even when I don't see your answers to my prayers.

Sarah said, "God has brought me laughter,
and everyone who hears about this
will laugh with me."

Genesis 21:6

Sarah

OUR SISTER SARAH knew how to laugh things off.

It was her safety valve. When something hurt or stung or brought up unbidden yesterdays, she would grab the string of humor, undoing the knots that looped and tangled.

One day she was looking up a cake recipe when she heard her name. What woman can resist eavesdropping when she hears her own name mentioned?

The oak tree committee was discussing her, it seemed. And what they said was ludicrous—a howl! Sarah would have a baby, they told her husband, Abraham.

Pablum and Pampers at ninety? Old enough for the rocking chair, yet rocking a baby? What kind of joke was this?

Sarah laughed so loudly that the three under the tree heard her. They brought the sudden sound to task before her husband. She stuck her head out the tent flap. "I did not laugh," she vowed. Then she pulled her head back before another spasm of mirth shook her body. Why, she'd passed the stage of hot flashes half a century ago!

Earlier in life, she had watched the calendar and day-dreamed about her apron hiding a secret. But then hope had taken a turn for the worse, growing weaker, more feeble. Her dream finally ended up as a corpse in the morgue of dead yearnings.

Sarah had been attractive all her life. Even as a child, she'd had a beauty pageant face with flawless skin a modern girl would trade her telephone for. Her eyes were clear, her hair shiny. She had a perfect nose and straight teeth that didn't need the discipline of hardware.

In her pre-bride days, she must have noticed that Abraham was a unique young man. He marched to higher notes than the rest. He was the moth that ate holes in the tarnished habits of the Chaldeans. He didn't go to the groves. He didn't pray to their gods. He wasn't even superstitious. Sarah decided that he was the man for her.

If ancient wedding vows called for loving, honoring, and obeying, Sarah gets an A+ on all three. A model wife, she never argued or backtalked. For several unrecorded years, Sarah didn't have to worry about "whither thou goest." Her husband was with the same company he had always worked for. She supposed he would retire with them.

Then, about the time she reached sixty-five, Abraham developed a fever for moving. He decided to follow a vision and look for an invisible city.

Sarah went along willingly. Abraham was right in her eyes...always. He was an altar builder. He loved God.

A hearty and practical woman, Sarah had stamina equal to the strain of travel. Like a military wife shipped to an unfamiliar post, she was ready to go on short notice. Following official orders, they would go where the food was different, the language was different, and the customs were different.

When the command came, Sarah hastily packed the U-Haul. Her commitment was for better or worse, richer or poorer, the plains of Mamre or the wells of Beersheba. She shared her husband's dangers with courage, his heartaches without complaint, and his dreams without criticism.

Who could have been a more perfect helpmate for the father of the faithful? He needed a plucky wife, and he got one.

In counting her blessings, Sarah came up only one short: she had no children. God had promised Abraham a son, so she believed and waited. But time ticked away. She started to panic. And when Sarah reached her seventy-fifth birthday, she began racing her motor.

We'd hardly dare call her impatient. But she decided something was amiss. No stork had migrated in their direction. Dream's deadline had passed. God had forgotten—or scrapped—his original plan. Maybe he had another woman in mind to mother this son?

So weary was Sarah of waiting—and so desperate for Abraham to have his boy—that she was willing to try anything, even a surrogate arrangement. She wanted to help God. She had forgotten that he is capable of carrying out his promises all by himself. He doesn't need human assistance.

Human help is as useless to God as a toothpick trying to prop up a skyscraper...and as apt to get squashed.

Reason said that if Sarah were ever to embrace a child, she would have to obtain him by proxy. Thus, in the game of life, she decided to move the chess pieces herself. Old age had already captured the queen.

She schemed to get a slave girl to bear Abraham's son. Her words may have said she believed God, but her actions said she didn't. When her plan came to birth, she learned a great lesson. She learned that one's own resources are not good enough to bring God's promises to fruition. Her idea was like baking bread without leaven. It fell flat and was hard to digest. It didn't taste right.

Unbelief can come up with a million alternatives, but Isaacs are not born by maneuvering around God's plan for the future. God's time seldom corresponds with Earth's, nor does his way.

Sarah felt that God was running late for his appointment. He hadn't shown up at age thirty. Or forty. Or fifty. But God is never late. He is not bound by time. The impossible is always possible for him. Hormones gone into hibernation certainly didn't frighten God.

Most of us can identify with Sarah's predicament. She had nothing to hold, to build upon. We've all been there. But with faith, one seldom has a check stub to show that the check has been written, that the answer is on the way. Faith is its own verification. God's Word stands collateral for itself.

Just ten years below the age of one hundred, Sarah breezed through natural childbirth, without classes on how to pant. She laughed again—a rich, bubbling laugh—and didn't try to suppress it.

"God has brought me laughter," she said. "And everyone who hears about this will laugh with me." Everybody was invited to join her in a good old-fashioned heehaw, to laugh with a gray-headed, diaper-changing, breast-feeding ninety-year-old who in our day would have made the *The Guinness Book of Records* as the world's oldest mom.

I find it amazing that Sarah didn't protest when her husband took her one and only son up the mountain to make a sacrifice of him. She had motherly feelings, prayed motherly prayers, and followed with her heart.

But she trusted this time. She had learned her faith lesson the hard way. She knew her son would be back. Abraham had used a plural pronoun when he spoke of their return. "We'll be back," he'd said.

In death, Sarah was still beautiful. She is the only woman in the Bible's four thousand year span whose length of life is recorded. She lived 127 full and rewarding years, each one sprinkled with laughter. She left behind a husband who never forgot her.

And the rest of us will never forget her either.

Just like Sarah, Lord, I panic when your promises seem delayed. Help me to remember that your plan will unfold in your time, better than I ever could have arranged it. Give me laughter, Lord, to release the tension. And help me to trust you more.

She said to her husband,
"I know that this man who often comes our way
is a holy man of God.
Let's make a small room on the roof and put in it
a bed and a table, a chair and a lamp for him.
Then he can stay there whenever he comes to us."

2 Kings 4:9-10

The Shunammite

THE HOSTESS OF THE YEAR award goes to our Shunammite sister.

Visitors were a pleasure, not an imposition. She didn't mind having another load for the washer or an extra meal to prepare. She liked pulling out the candles, setting out the snack trays, and using scented sheets in the guest room.

Her name is never mentioned. But that doesn't matter. One adjective describes her well:

Great.

She was great in heart, great in kindness, and great in generosity.

She had one of those neat cottages beside the road. In the background, Mount Carmel climbed to the cobalt sky. There were flower beds and a little garden. Perhaps a picket fence.

In the Shunammite's day, there were few accommodations for travelers. "Bed and Breakfast" meant a friend's house. YMCA's were unheard of. There was no Salvation Army. There were no rescue missions. There wasn't even a jailhouse to lodge transients overnight.

Instead of turning traveling preachers away, the Shunammite simply asked her husband to build an extra room. Carefully and cheerfully she decorated it. She furnished it for comfort at her own expense. It had a table. A stool. A candlestick. A bed.

She especially liked to keep heaven's ambassadors, and the prophet Elisha made her add-on room his home away from home. He was comfortable there and knew he'd be welcomed as a drop-in. He didn't even have to phone ahead.

The lady proved to be an ideal hostess, so the prophet asked what she would like as a reward for all her hot biscuits and molasses. Reward? A reward had never crossed her mind. The joys of entertaining a prophet were enough.

"But isn't there something you'd like?" he asked. An introduction to the president? An invitation to tea at the White House? Her name on the First Lady's mailing list?

But the woman was satisfied with her simple life. Her family lived close by. Her home was paid for. They were in good health. What more could one ask?

However, Elisha wasn't satisfied that his debt go unpaid. He—and God—would not let such kindness go unrewarded. Surely there must be some way to compensate this thoughtful woman for her hospitality.

Elisha's servant was a perceptive soul. He looked around, but saw no high chair, no playpen, no port-a-crib. There were no children's pictures on the wall. So he suggested to his master that their hostess might like a tyke around the place. After all, he noted, her husband *was* getting on in years.

Elisha called the woman back. She stood in the door and tried to comprehend the prophet's idea of a reward. She begged him not to tease her. That was a sensitive spot in her life. She'd tried to use good deeds to fill the empty arms that ached to hold a child.

But nine months later, her precious gift came.

Did she close off Elisha's room and send him elsewhere so she could care for the nursery? No. Even as a new mother, she still found time to be hospitable. To fluff pillows. To fill water pitchers. To bake cookies.

Her greatness passed the motherhood test, too.

Then one day, Mr. Shunammite brought the little Shunammite home to his mother. The boy had stayed out in the field too long. Now, he was hot, and had taken a bad headache.

His mother held him and tried to bring his fever down with cool rags. She prayed for him, then checked the thermometer. She sang to him, then checked the thermometer. She told him stories, then checked the thermometer.

But the boy grew worse. His breath came slower, then not at all. His mother's heart almost stopped with his. She wished it could. The gracious woman had lost her greatest treasure.

She kept her head and pondered what to do. As she carried her son to the guest room, she walked through the same door where she had stood when Elisha had promised her the child. She placed the boy on Elisha's bed: the same bed that had been slept on by the man who had offered her the reward. The room symbolized a great man who served a great God, and now this great woman needed a great miracle.

So she shut the door on her troubles and left, telling her husband she was making an unexpected journey to see the prophet. "Why today?" he wanted to know. It wasn't a new moon. Or Sabbath. It wasn't church time.

"Everything will be okay," she said. Then she turned to the donkey driver and urged him to put the beast in overdrive. Stay off the brakes, she begged. Ignore the speed limits. Take no detours. There's no stopping at roadside parks or historical markers, no dallying to take pictures.

Just go!

Elisha saw a cloud squatting on the horizon like a dust devil. He shaded his eyes to see better.

The Shunammite. Was she well? Was her husband ill? What about her child? He sent his servant as his roving reporter to interview her.

It is well, she told the hired man. A brave vest of words, but not quite bullet-proof for her quaking heart. Elisha knew better. Something was wrong and God had him blindfolded.

The woman fell at Elisha's feet, clutching them in a desperate grip. The prophet's servant tried to shoo her away, but Elisha held up his hand. They must leave her alone, he said, until they could determine what had her in such a stew.

When the truth tumbled out, Elisha sent his helper sizzling to Shunem with instructions. The servant was to take his master's walking stick with him and not say hello to anyone along the way. When he arrived at the woman's home, he was to lay the cane on the boy's face.

Meanwhile, Elisha followed Mrs. Shunammite back down the path she had come, back toward Shunem. They met the servant coming back. He had obeyed orders, he said. But nothing had happened. The boy was no better.

Elisha found the boy dead on Elisha's own guest bed. He shut the door and prayed, then gave the child mouth-to-mouth resuscitation. Some of the cold left the body, starting a warming trend.

Elisha paced the floor, then tried artificial respiration again.

"A-choo!" It happened seven times. The boy sneezed and sneezed. And sneezed some more. As he opened his eyes and saw Elisha, he tried on a small smile that just fit.

Elisha sent for the worried mother and presented her child to her, ready to go again: full steam ahead. Just like her hospitality.

For kindness will always find its way home.

Lord, you are the author of all generosity. Give me opportunities to share your kindness with others. Teach me to honor you with my actions. And make me an example of your goodness.

Charm is deceptive, and beauty is fleeting;
but a woman who fears the LORD is to be praised.

Proverbs 31:30

The Virtuous Woman

THERE'S ONE in every family.

We couldn't get through life without one sister to show us up. She's the one who wins it all, leaving us feeling like footnotes in a library book.

King Lemuel's virtuous woman of Proverbs 31—the one his mother told him about—was perfect. She was voted B.C. 1015's top of the top ten. The honor came complete with halo and wings.

She is constantly being held up to women as a shining example. (That's why sisters were invented.) "Look what she did! Look how she did it!" She got merit awards in every subject.

"Why can't you be like your sister?" Ah, wishful thinking! Some of us aren't so organized. So indefatigable. So talented.

The average woman doesn't have a price tag dangling from her neck, saying "more expensive than rubies." Most of us would be better compared to a nugget of ice cream salt on a bargain counter. We'd all like to be as praise-worthy as our flawless sister, but the fabric from which we're cut comes up a whole yard short.

We are reminded that she got up before daylight to prepare breakfast for her family and all the hired help. She made hot biscuits and the other 4:00 a.m. courses, minus a microwave oven. She didn't plop down a bowl of cereal and say, "There! Like it or lump it." She didn't tolerate second-rate food. It had to be top quality. Gourmet.

Miles or kilometers meant nothing to her. She traveled great distances to get the best money could buy to grace her table. She didn't even have a car with a fuel-injected engine, power steering and power brakes, or an air condi-tioner and heater.

A seamstress she was, of the highest order. She knew where to put darts and how to backstitch and which pat-tern would look right on whom. She could crochet, em-broider, knit and tat, quilt and smock, applique and monogram. She'd even tackle crawly material like silk, or thick wool.

She upholstered her own furniture sans a computer-ized sewing machine. But that's not the half of it. She *made money* on her fancy handwork. It was in demand. She wove fine linen and made girdles. The dry goods stores snapped them up.

All this is beside her real estate business, which turned enough profit to make Century 21 sit up and take notice. She took out an ad in the Yellow Pages, studied the market, and bought land. Then she transmogrified it into a Garden of Eden and sold it.

The woman had self-confidence. She didn't crack her knuckles or hector a strand of hair. She knew that what she did and what she sold was Cadillac competition.

But that's not all. We must not overlook the fact that she was into charity, too. Hospital visitation. Benevolent collections. Funeral dinners.

She could have supper in and out of the oven in the time it takes us to find the recipe. And she could do it all with time left over to play tennis, tole paint, and exercise.

Whew!

Naturally, her husband was proud of her. He was recognized at the gates, at the city council, and at the Lion's Club. He was Wonder Woman's husband. There was no pumpkin-shell wife here.

Even her children complimented her. She had no dread of weather, hot or cold. She kept the light burning all night like Motel 6. She was so proper, she makes the rest of us look sick. We hope our husbands never look her way and see what they're missing. Her words were gilded with finesse. She handled her PR work just right.

We'll have to agree with Lemuel's mother that the bread of idleness wasn't in this sister's dictionary. Just thinking about her boundless energy makes us under-achievers tired.

So how can we still love our goody-goody sister when the backdrop of her achievements makes our puny accomplishments look so small? We can do it because all of us need an ideal and a heroine. She is our mentor, our sampler.

We can admire her foremost for her beautiful attitude. She didn't complain, like a martyr. She didn't nag or brag.

One who lives such a full life must be acquainted with fatigue. She was a dust-made female like ourselves. Her hands—at one time or another—grew weary, her eyes heavy. But she *enjoyed* what she was contributing to her family, society, and the world at large.

Patience made her gracious.

Hope made her happy.

Love made her strong.

We can sit in the audience and applaud. We know she's Oscar-deserving. She is a sister we can be proud of and gloat over. Her bio is hard to live up to, but it makes us work a little harder, causes us to stand a little taller.

And inspires us to try again and again.

Lord, help me not to become overwhelmed by the achievements of my virtuous sister. Instead, let me be inspired by her unselfish devotion. I know that my accomplishments don't have to be the same as hers. Thank you for the unique talents and gifts you have given me. And please help me to use them well.